READY TO LEARN

First Grade

Workbook

Table of Contents

READY TO LEARN
First Grade

A NOTE TO PARENTS, CAREGIVERS, AND TEACHERS

The *Ready to Learn* series is an excellent tool for assisting your child, grandchild, or student in developing readiness skills in mathematics, reading, and writing during his or her early learning years. The colorful and engaging workbooks, workpads, and flash cards support the acquisition of foundational skills that all children need to be successful in school and everyday life.

The *Ready to Learn* series develops skills targeted to the Common Core State Standards. The practice workbooks include explanations, strategies, and practice opportunities that engage your young learner with the building blocks needed to become a confident mathematician, reader, and writer. The workpads provide additional practice for the key concepts addressed in the workbooks, and the flash cards support fluency in basic math and reading concepts.

Ready to Learn workbooks include an overview page to inform adults of the learning objectives inside, as well as a certificate at the end of the book to present to your child or student upon completion of the workbook. It is recommended that you display each certificate earned in a prominent location where your child or student can proudly share with others that he or she is excited to be a learner!

While the *Ready to Learn* series is designed to support your child's or student's acquisition of foundational skills, it is important that you practice these skills beyond the series. Encourage your child or student to find examples of what he or she has learned in various environments, such as letters and words on menus at a restaurant, numbers at a grocery store, and colors and shapes on the playground.

Thank you for caring about your child or student's education.
Happy learning!

Reading

Table of Contents

First grade is when children can bloom into readers by following simple strategies to help them use the sight words and letter-and-sound knowledge that they learned in kindergarten. Taking these skills to the next level will take practice, but practice can be fun! Help your child through the activities in this book and watch him or her grow into a successful reader.

What Good Readers Do:

1. Read every day.

2. Read everything around them.

3. Choose "just right" books.

4. Use strategies to help with words they don't know.

5. Think about what they read.

6. Make connections to what they read.

7. Make predictions about what they read.

8. Ask questions when they read.

Good readers read every day and read everything around them. There is so much to read! There are letters, numbers, words, signs, posters, books, grocery lists, and so much more. Protect your reading time. It is important to read, read, read every day!

Reading is fun and the stories you read can take you on amazing adventures. There are...

3 Ways to Read a Book

• Read the words.

• Look at the pictures to help you figure out the words.

• Retell what you read to a friend.

What is your favorite book? Write the title on the lines below.

_____

_____

Go get that favorite book and have fun reading!

Choosing a Book That Is "Just Right" for You

Books are like shoes. Not everyone can wear the same size shoes. Make sure the book you are reading is not too difficult or too easy to read. Follow these simple steps to choose a book that is the right fit for you.

Use the five finger rule to help choose a just right book.

Five Finger Rule

Choose a book. Open it to any page.
Put one finger up for each
word you don't know.

0–1 fingers Too easy
2–3 fingers Just right
4 fingers   Give it a try
5+ fingers   Too hard

Look at the Pictures

A word is missing in each sentence below. Read the sentences and use the pictures as clues to help you decide what each missing word is. Circle the correct missing word and write it on the lines below.

The cat is up the ___tree___.
(tree or top)

The boy has a ___sandwich___.
(shoe or (sandwich))

I like to play ___soccer___.
(baseball or soccer)

My mom likes to ___cook___.
(cook or jump)

She is riding the ___bike___.
(bus or (bike))

Picture Clues

A word is missing in each sentence below. Read the sentences and use the pictures as clues to help you decide what each missing word is. Circle the correct missing word and write it on the lines below.

I saw _____ at the zoo.
(fish or animals)

I saw _____ at the farm.
(pigs or lions)

I had an _____ for lunch.
(orange or apple)

I take the _____ to school.
(bus or canoe)

I had a birthday _____.
(chair or cake)

Initial Sounds

Look at the pictures. Write the missing letters to complete the words below.
Then read the words.

_b_oy

_r_un

_p_ig

_b_aby

_t_able

_c_at

_l_etter

_f_rog

_g_oat

Decoding Strategies

Initial Sounds

Read the words in the pictures below.

Color the flowers with words that begin with the letter j.

Color the balloons with words that begin with the letter b.

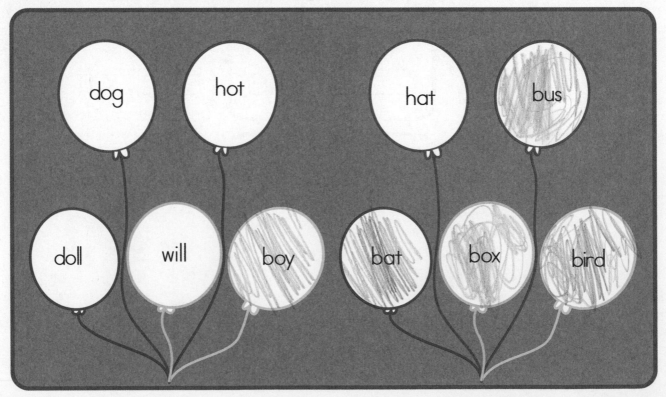

Decoding Strategies

Medial Sounds

Look at the pictures. Write the missing letters to complete the words below.

b___d

h___t

h___n

c___t

n___t

l___g

s___n

t___p

b___s

Medial Sounds

Write the missing vowels to complete each word below. Then draw a line to match the object on the left to its opposite on the right.

l_i_ttle

h_o_t

s___mmer

w_i_nter

c_o_ld

l__ng

sh_o_rt

b__g

Decoding Strategies

Looking for "Chunks"

Some chunks are called rimes or word families because the words will rhyme. Write a letter on each line below to create a word family. Color the snakes.

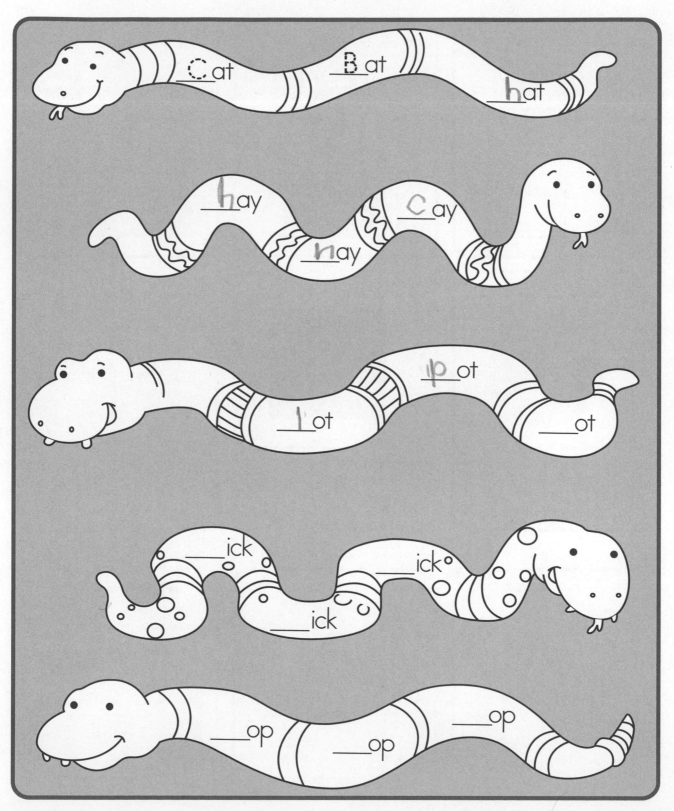

Decoding Strategies

Final Sounds with Double Consonants

Some words end with two of the same letter. Look at the pictures and complete the words by writing the missing double consonants on the lines below.

be_ _ _ _

do_ _ _ _ _

e_ _ _ _ _

ba_ _ _ _ _

wa_ _ _ _ _

a_ _ _ _ _

gra_ _ _ _ _

dre_ _ _ _ _

pu_ _ _ _ _

Decoding Strategies

Looking for "Chunks"

Recognizing parts of words can help you sound out words faster. Look for "chunks" in the words you read.

Circle the words below that have the chunk shown on the left.

sh	share	chick	show
ch	chip	chin	this
th	that	when	there
at	shop	mat	bat
an	man	tan	cat
ack	rack	barn	sack
ip	top	sip	slip
ill	bill	fill	fall
op	mop	him	stop
ut	hut	hit	nut

Flipping the Vowel

Long Vowel Sounds

Write the missing vowels to complete each story. Then read the stories.

Come out to pl___y.

It is a sunny d___y.

What do you s___y?

I grew out of my tr___ke.

I now have a b___ke.

It is what I l___ke.

Decoding Strategies

Context Clues and Picture Clues

Sometimes trying to figure out a word by sounding it out may not help you. If this happens, try skipping the word and reading the rest of the sentence to see if you can figure out the word. Does the sentence sound right? Does it make sense? Another clue to help you figure out an unknown word is to look at the pictures on the page you are reading.

A word is missing in each sentence below. Read the sentences. Use the other words in the sentences and the pictures to help you figure out the missing words. Write the missing words on the lines below.

The _____ is on the log.

I can ride a _____ .

I see a cow near the _____ .

The cat has a red _____ .

I can climb a _____ .

Sight Words

Words to Practice and Know

There are some words that are difficult to sound out and that do not have picture clues. Reading and remembering them can make reading easier. Practice reading these sight words until you recognize them when you see them in books.

the	no	look	came
is	like	so	down
in	my	do	them
it	what	she	would
to	were	an	could
I	when	said	went
he	come	can	her
at	have	not	am
be	some	but	get
we	into	up	want

all	his	here	your
had	as	little	did
saw	on	make	about
this	for	yes	many
they	see	then	look
with	you	out	very
are	a	will	has
was	and	go	from
that	of	if	use
by	or	there	first

Sight Words

Find and circle the sight words below using different colors for each word. Then fill in the graph by coloring one box for every sight word you find. Write the total number of words you find next to the graph on the lines below.

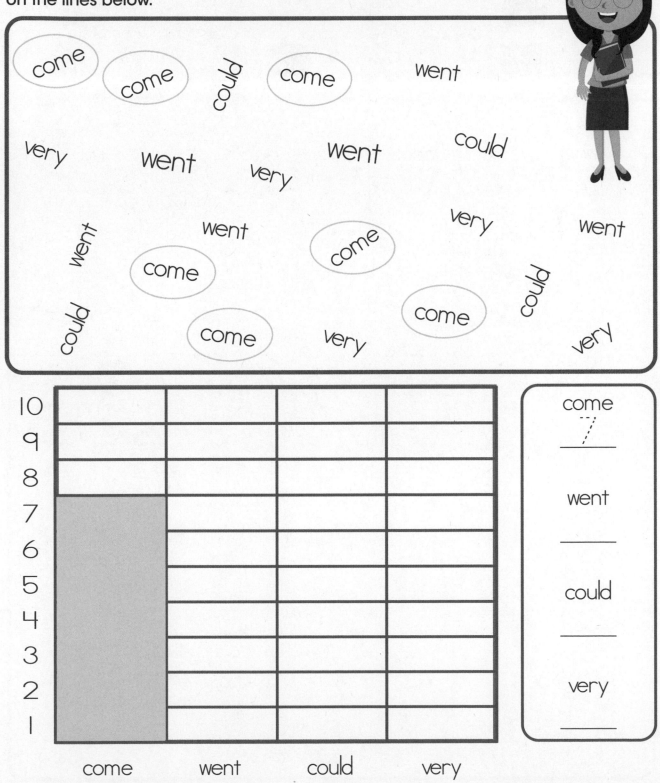

Sight Words

Color the pumpkins below using the key.

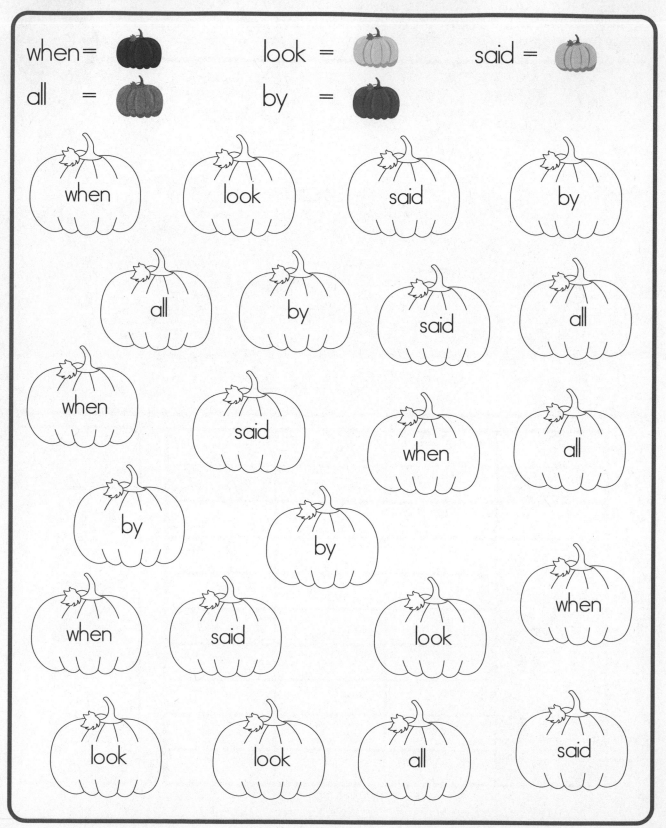

when =
look =
said =
all =
by =

when   look   said   by

all   by   said   all

when   said   when   all

by   by

when   said   look   when

look   look   all   said

Sight Words

Color the picture below using the key.

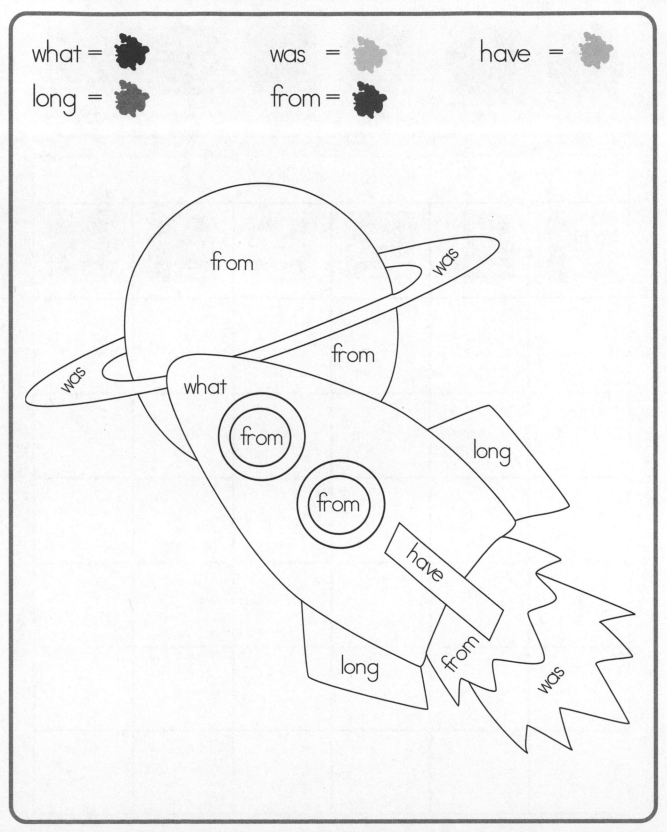

Sight Words

Roll a die and use the key to write the corresponding sight word in the correct column. Roll until the grid is full.

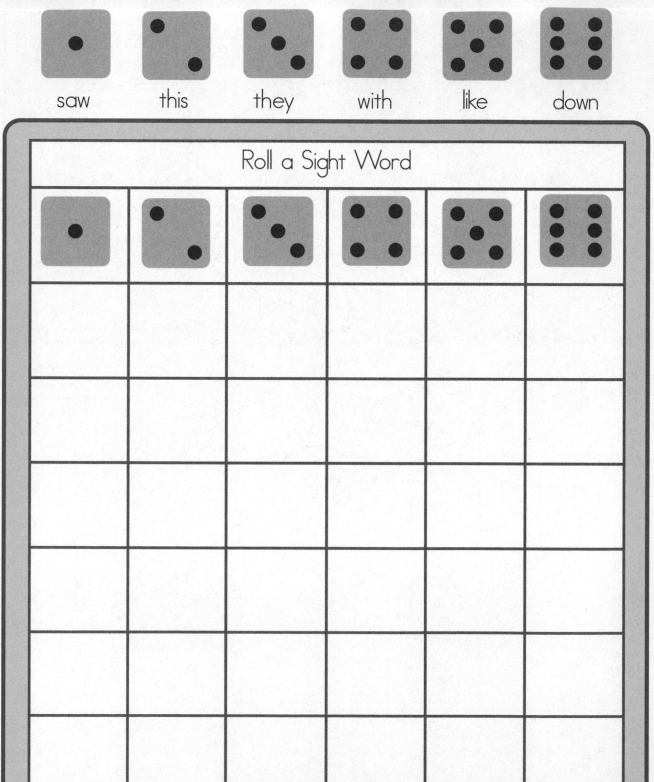

saw · this · they · with · like · down

Roll a Sight Word

Sight Word Activities

Sight Words

Complete the word search below by finding and circling all the sight words listed in the box. Words may be horizontal, vertical, or diagonal, but they will all be forwards—no backwards words allowed!

Search for the following words:

and	out	make	in	it
my	she	about	this	if

O	E	H	K	T	H	I	S	C	H	K
U	B	C	G	A	G	P	G	R	I	M
T	C	B	A	H	K	B	O	N	C	N
F	D	C	G	M	J	I	T	A	L	C
I	B	H	A	E	A	P	S	W	A	X
H	E	T	N	I	B	K	C	V	F	U
O	M	E	D	F	R	S	E	N	K	E
F	B	F	G	P	Q	H	M	A	L	G
N	R	A	N	J	O	E	D	I	G	J
O	A	W	L	G	S	I	F	X	Y	Z
M	Y	I	J	Q	B	K	O	F	C	Y
O	A	B	O	U	T	F	L	E	I	X

Read the sentences below. The sight words are underlined. Use the reading strategies you have learned to read the other words.

He can sip from the cup.

I like my red shoes.

The cat is not fat.

The dog ran home.

Read the sentences below. The sight words are underlined. Use the reading strategies you have learned to read the other words.

How many cats do you see?

She loves jumping rope.

I have a pet goat.

The frog is on the log.

Rhymes and Rhyming Words

Words That Rhyme

Words that rhyme have the same ending sound. Circle the words that rhyme. Then color the pictures.

Take my hand
and we will sit on the sand,
while we hear the best band
in all of the land.

Hooray! Hooray!
What a beautiful day.
We can swim in the bay,
and catch a sun ray.

Rhymes and Rhyming Words

Words That Rhyme
Circle the words that rhyme. Then color the picture.

Oh rats! I just saw three cats
wearing three aprons
and three floppy hats!

What a funny sight!
These dogs like to write,
but only at night.
Are you sure that is right?

Word Meanings

Read the story below.

Halloween Night

It was raining on Halloween night. I was feeling disappointed. I had a great monster costume. I got dressed up anyway. I jumped out and surprised my dad and frightened him. Finally, the rain stopped and my dad took me trick-or-treating.

Read the questions below about the story and circle the correct answers.

In the story, the word "disappointed" means:

a. scared   b. happy   c. sad

The word "frightened" means:

a. happy   b. scared   c. sad

The word "finally" means:

a. at last   b. first   c. before

Word Meanings

Read the story below.

The Circus

I can't believe it happened! I was at the circus with my mom. A tiger let out a huge roar. The magician was doing tricks. Then a clown picked me out of the audience to help. The magician made me disappear!

Read the questions below about the story and circle the correct answers.

In the story, the word "huge" means:

a. small   b. very big   c. tiny

The word "audience" means:

a. a loud noise   b. people watching a show   c. tired

The word "disappear" means:

a. turn purple   b. can't be seen   c. get really
                                                          hungry

Word Meanings

Read the story below.

Our New Car

My mom got a new car. The paint is crimson. She uses the vacuum every day to keep it clean. She is really proud of her new car.

Read the questions below about the story and circle the correct answers.

The word "crimson" means:

a. shiny   b. red   c. big

The word "vacuum" means:

a. a cleaning tool   b. a toy   c. a pet

The word "proud" means:

a. feeling happy   b. feeling sad   c. feeling afraid

The Cover

The cover is an important part of a book. It is the first thing a reader sees. It helps the reader decide if he or she is interested in the book.

Use the information above to answer the questions. Write your answers on the lines below.

What is the book about?

_____

_____

Who drew the pictures in the book?

_____

_____

Who wrote the words in the book?

_____

_____

Text and Illustrations

The inside of books can look different. Some books have pictures and others just have words. Most of the books read in first grade have both!

Use the picture and sentences in the book to answer the questions. Write your answers on the lines below.

Is it daytime or nighttime? How do you know?

_____

_____

_____

_____

_____

_____

_____

_____

Characters

Characters are the people, animals, or other creatures in the story.

Color the characters in the picture below.

Setting

The setting is where a story takes place.

Look at the pictures. Then draw a line from the picture to the name of the setting.

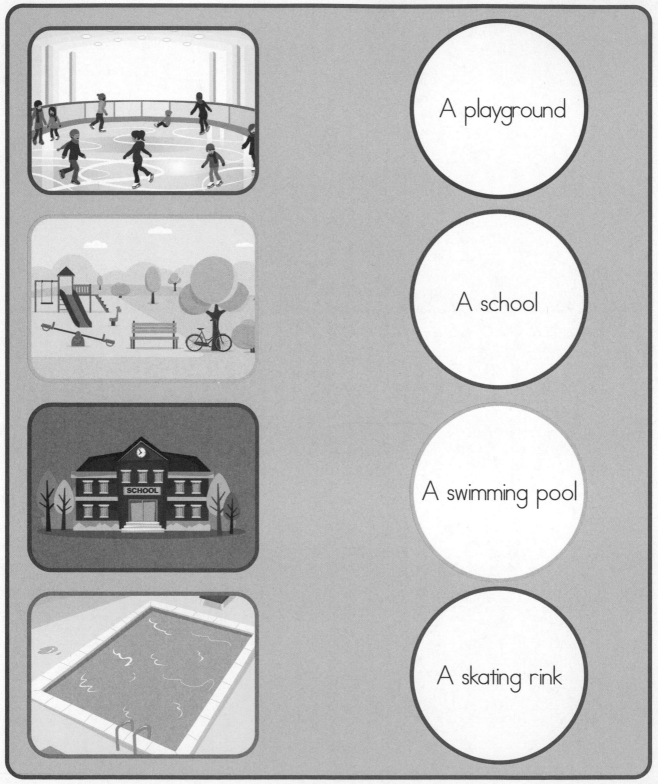

A playground

A school

A swimming pool

A skating rink

Problem and Solution

The problem in a story is something that happens that needs to be fixed.
The solution in a story is how the problem is solved.

Look at the picture and use your reading strategies to read the sentences and answer the questions. Write your answers on the lines below.

Kristin and Zac wanted macaroni and cheese for dinner. When they started cooking, they didn't have any cheese. Mom went to the store to get some. They all had macaroni and cheese for dinner that night.

What is the problem in the story?

_____

_____

_____

_____

_____

What is the solution?

_____

_____

_____

_____

_____

Problem and Solution

Read the problems below and draw a line to the picture that shows the solution.

Pat missed the bus.

Liam forgot his lunch at home.

Sammy keeps tripping on her shoelaces.

Lucas spilled his glass of milk.

Maya fell and scraped her knee.

Sequencing

Read the story below.

At the Park

I went to play with my friend at the park. We played on the slide. We played tag. We played on the swings. We had so much fun at the park.

Draw a line from the picture to the order the event happens in the story.

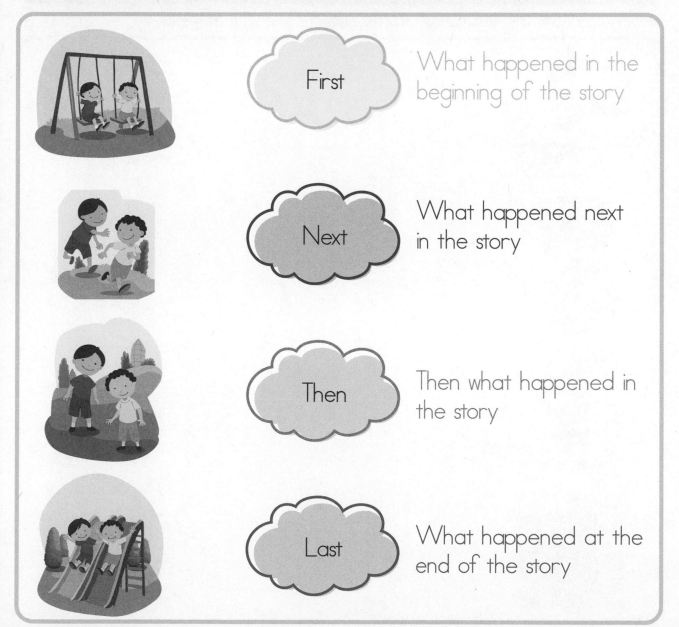

First — What happened in the beginning of the story

Next — What happened next in the story

Then — Then what happened in the story

Last — What happened at the end of the story

37

Sequencing

Read the story below.

Maggie's Day Out

Hi! My name is Maggie. I am a dog. The other day I left my house and went for a run. I saw a cat and chased it down the street. When I got hungry, I went home for dinner. What a great day!

Draw a line from the illustrations to the order of events in the story.

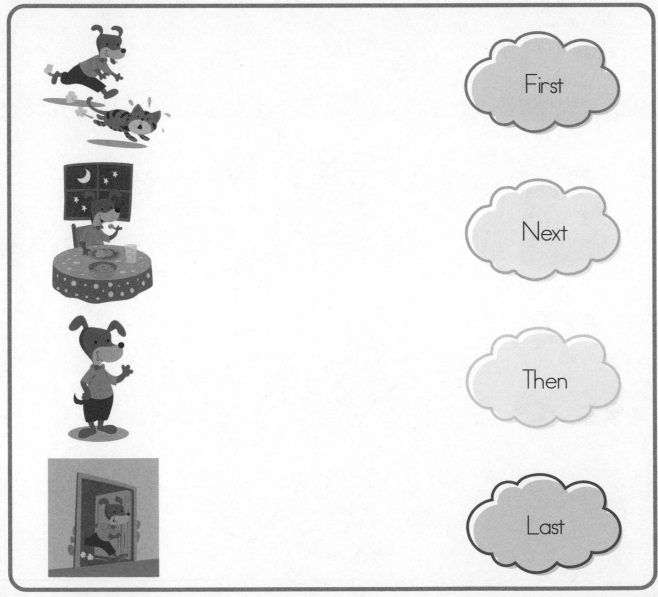

First

Next

Then

Last

Sequencing

Read the story below.

The Big Ship

The big ship is anchored to the dock. Machines unload big metal boxes onto trucks. The ship blows its loud horn. Then the big ship pulls away from the dock.

Draw a line from the illustrations to the order of events in the story.

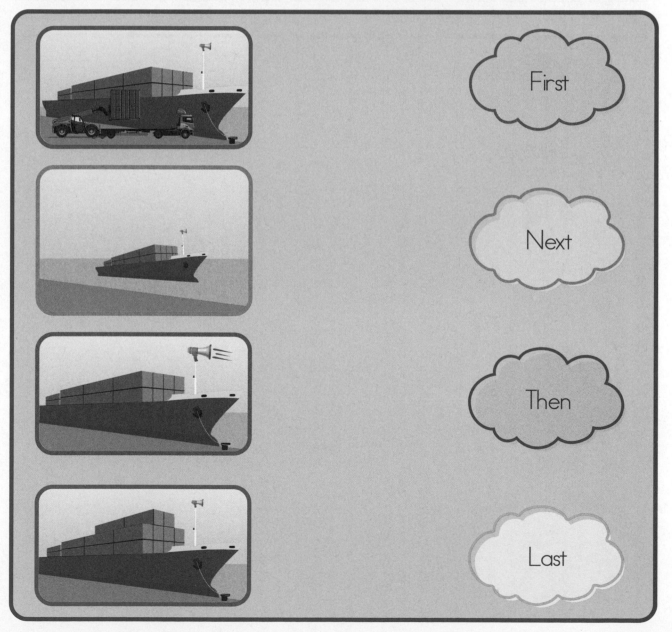

First

Next

Then

Last

Sequencing

Read the story below.

Making a Cake

I made a cake today! My mom and I mixed the batter in a bowl. I licked the spoon. We poured the batter in a cake pan and put it in the oven. When it was done, we put icing on the cake. It was delicious. YUM!

Draw a line from the illustrations to the order of events in the story.

First

Next

Then

Last

The cover of a book can help you predict what the book is about.

- The title and the illustration give you a hint.
- The author's name might even give you a hint if you have read a book written by them before.

Use the information above to predict what this book is about. Write your answer on the lines below.

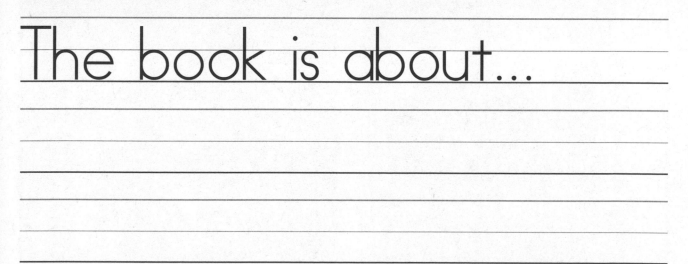

The book is about...

Making Predictions

Use the cover to make predictions about the book. Draw a line from the book cover to your prediction.

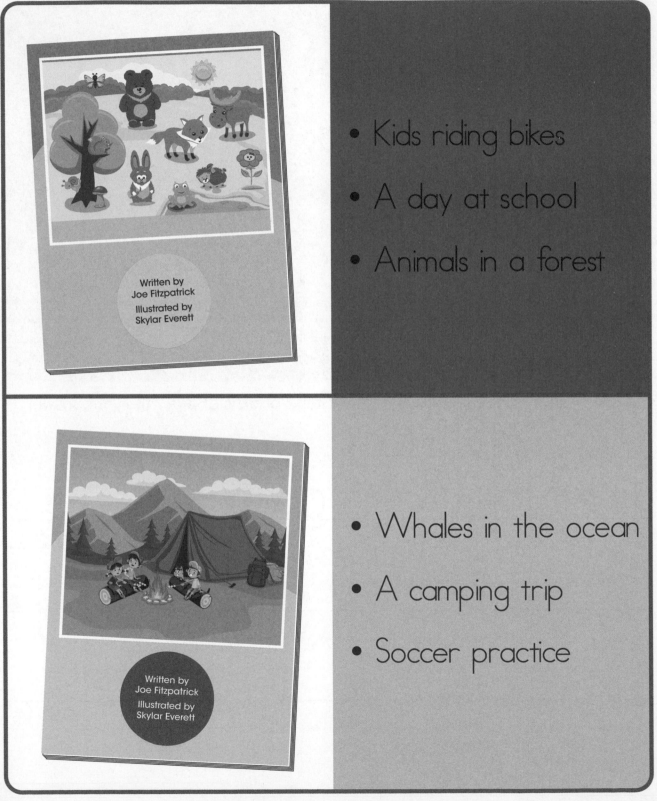

Written by
Joe Fitzpatrick

Illustrated by
Skylar Everett

- Kids riding bikes

- A day at school

- Animals in a forest

Written by
Joe Fitzpatrick

Illustrated by
Skylar Everett

- Whales in the ocean

- A camping trip

- Soccer practice

Making Predictions

Make predictions as you read.

Read the story below.

The Triple Cactus

Zac was riding his skateboard. He was doing lots of tricks. Zac was great at doing tricks. He decided to try one he had never done before. It was called the triple cactus.

On the lines below, write what you think will happen next.

_____

_____

_____

_____

_____

_____

_____

_____

Visualizing What You Read

Reading a story can paint a picture in your mind. Close your eyes and think about a birthday cake. Do you have a picture in your mind of what it looks like? That is visualizing!

Read the sentences below and draw a picture of what you imagine.

It is my birthday.
I cannot wait for my party!

Reading Comprehension

Visualizing What You Read

Read the sentences below and draw a picture of what you imagine.

My dad is taking me to the game this weekend. I am so excited!

Visualizing What You Read

Read the sentence below and draw a picture of what you imagine.

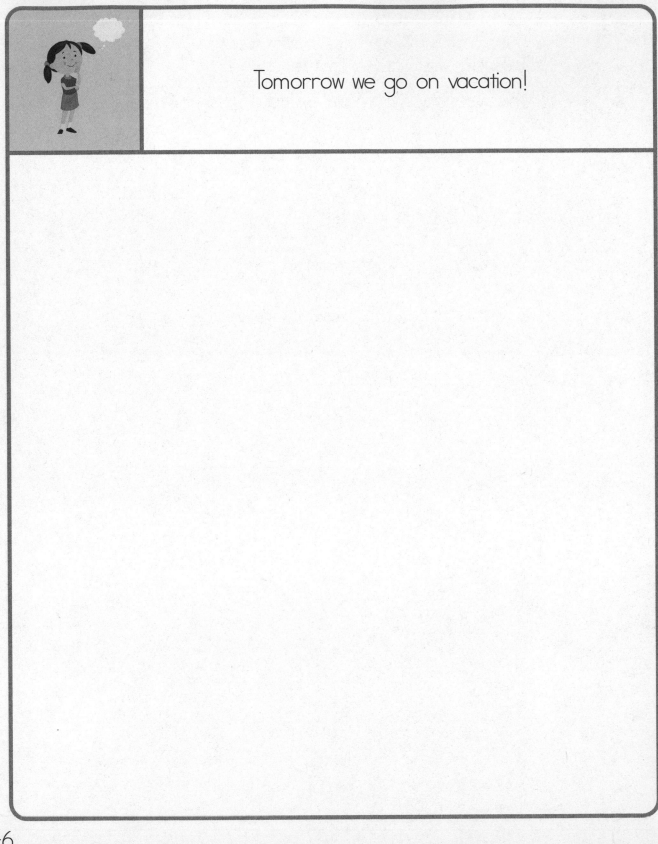

Tomorrow we go on vacation!

Visualizing What You Read

Read the sentence below and draw a picture of what you imagine.

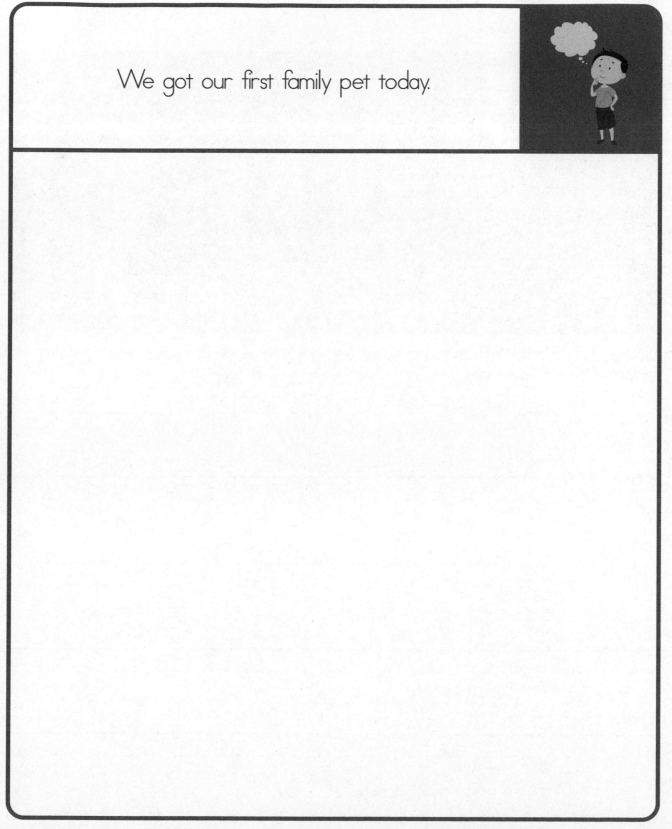

We got our first family pet today.

Making Connections

When something in a story reminds you of something that happened to you, you are making a connection to the story!

Read the story below.

The Loose Tooth

I had an apple for lunch today. When I bit into my apple, I felt something pop. I moved my tongue around in my mouth and felt a loose tooth! I wiggled it all day long thinking it would come out, but it didn't. When I got home, I showed my mom and she had an idea.

Do you feel a connection to the story? Have you ever had a loose tooth? Write about it on the lines below.

_____

_____

_____

_____

_____

_____

_____

_____

_____

_____

_____

Making Connections

Read the story below.

Melissa and the Three Bunnies

One day, Melissa was walking in the forest when she saw a little house. She decided to go in to see who was home. On the table she saw three carrots. She was very hungry and decided to eat one. The big carrot was too hot. The small carrot was too cold. The medium carrot was just right.

Do you feel a connection to the story? Does this story remind you of any other stories you have read? Have you ever been very hungry? Write about it on the lines below.

_____

_____

_____

_____

_____

_____

_____

_____

_____

_____

_____

Understanding What You Read Using Clues

Look at each picture and read the sentences. Circle the sentence that matches the picture and then write it on the lines below.

The boy is making a cake.
The girl is painting the fence.

The farmer is milking the cow.
The man is chopping down the tree.

The pig is in the barn.
The horse jumped over the fence.

The girl is reading a book.
The boys are playing tag.

Understanding What You Read Using Clues

Use the clues to find out who each character is. Draw a line from the character to his or her name.

Connor is wearing a red shirt. He likes to play soccer.

Gabby plays with her baby doll.

Max loves to read.

Kate loves to pick flowers.

Max

Gabby

Kate

Connor

Reading Comprehension

Understanding What You Read Using Clues

Read the sentences and color the picture that matches the clues.

I walk sideways.

I have claws.

I love to go for walks and play fetch.

I have four legs.

I live on a farm.

I make milk.

I love to eat carrots.

I have long ears.

Understanding What You Read Using Clues
Read the sentences below.

Hannah is wearing a pink top. Jane is wearing a green skirt with a green top. Jane always wears a bow in her hair to match her top. Ben has curly hair and is wearing a blue sweater and blue jeans. Kurt has brown hair and it is the same color as his jacket. Jacob has red hair that matches his favorite shoes.

Color the picture to match the sentences. Then, on the lines below, answer the questions about what you read.

How many kids are waiting for the school bus?_____
Who is first in line?_____
Who is last in line?_____

Following Directions

Read the directions below and color the picture.

1. Color the bush to the left of the house green.
2. Color the sun yellow.
3. Color the chimney on the roof red.
4. Color the windows light blue.
5. Draw some fluffy clouds in the sky.
6. Draw three flowers near the tree.
7. Color the door red.
8. Color the leaves on the tree green.
9. Color the rest of the house any color you like.

Following Directions

Read the sentences below and complete the picture.

1. Draw a beach umbrella for the family.
2. Draw a boat on the water.
3. Draw a sun in the sky.
4. Draw a kite in the sky.
5. Draw a crab on the sand.
6. Draw a pail and shovel on the beach.
7. Draw a beach ball.
8. Draw yourself on the beach.

Seasons

Read the poem below. Then color the pictures.

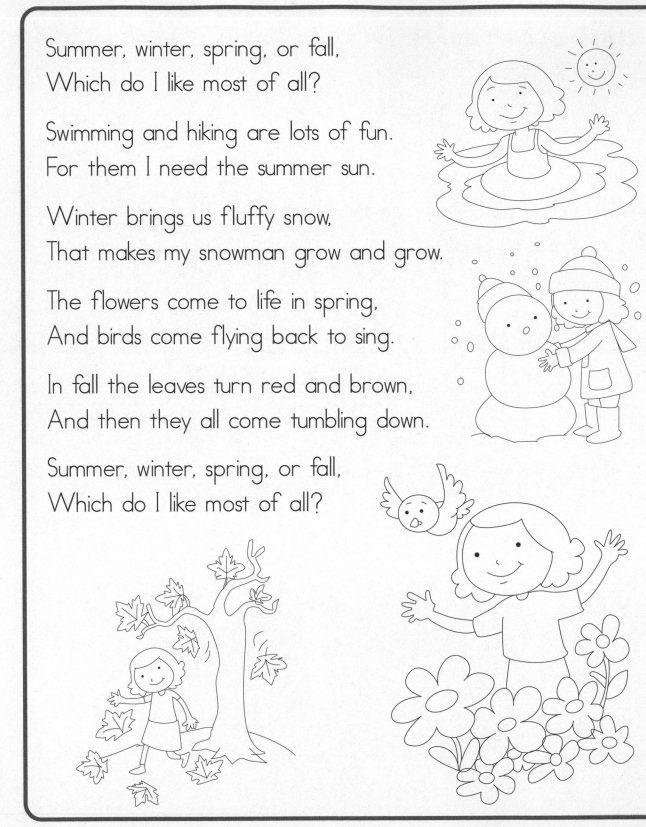

Summer, winter, spring, or fall,
Which do I like most of all?

Swimming and hiking are lots of fun.
For them I need the summer sun.

Winter brings us fluffy snow,
That makes my snowman grow and grow.

The flowers come to life in spring,
And birds come flying back to sing.

In fall the leaves turn red and brown,
And then they all come tumbling down.

Summer, winter, spring, or fall,
Which do I like most of all?

Climbing Trees

Read the story below. Then color the picture.

Ella and Finn like to climb trees. They see a kitten in the tree. The kitten is afraid. It will not come down. Finn tries to help the kitten. The kitten climbs higher up the tree. Ella pats the kitten and picks it up. Finn and Ella are good climbers. They are good helpers, too!

Comic Strip Fun

Read the comic strip below.

Soccer

Read the story below. Then color the picture.

Hector is going to play soccer today.

He is very happy.

He likes to play soccer.

After the game begins, it starts to rain.

The kids keep playing anyway.

It got very muddy! It was a lot of fun!

Riddles

Riddles are brain teasers that make you think. Read the riddles below and try to answer them. Then color the pictures.

1. I am full of holes, but I can still hold water.
    What am I?_____

2. I have hands and a face, but I can't touch or smile.
    What am I? _____

3. I get wetter and wetter the more I dry.
    What am I? _____

4. I have lots of keys but can't open any door.
    What am I? _____

Compound Words

Compound words are two words that make a new word when they are put together. Look at the pictures to figure out the compound words. Write the words on the lines below.

CERTIFICATE
of Achievement

....

has successfully completed
1st Grade Reading

Signed:

Date:

Writing

Table of Contents

First Grade Writing Readiness

In first grade, children are fine-tuning their letter formation and becoming creative writers. Throughout this workbook, children will learn how to brainstorm for writing and how to write for different purposes. Give your child every opportunity they can to be writers. Set up a writing corner with paper, pencils, crayons, and other writing supplies, and watch your child become a proud author!

Aa

Practice writing the uppercase letter A on the lines below.

Practice writing the lowercase letter a on the lines below.

Write the words apple, acorn, and antelope on the lines below.

apple _____   acorn _____

antelope _____

Color the pictures that begin with the letter A.

Letter Formation

Bb

Practice writing the uppercase letter B on the lines below.

Practice writing the lowercase letter b on the lines below.

Write the words ball, bear, and butterfly on the lines below.

ball

bear

butterfly

Draw three pictures that begin with the letter B.

66

Cc
Practice writing the uppercase letter C on the lines below.

C ⟳¹ ⟲ (dotted C)

Practice writing the lowercase letter c on the lines below.

c ⟳¹ (dotted c)

Write the words cat, cow, and caterpillar on the lines below.

cat

cow

caterpillar

Circle the pictures that begin with the letter C.

Dd

Practice writing the uppercase letter D on the lines below.

Practice writing the lowercase letter d on the lines below.

Write the words dog, dig, and dinosaur on the lines below.

dog

dig

dinosaur

Circle the pictures that begin with the letter D.

Ee

Practice writing the uppercase letter E on the lines below.

Practice writing the lowercase letter e on the lines below.

Write the words elf, ear, and elephant on the lines below.

elf

ear

elephant

Color the pictures that begin with the letter E.

Ff

Practice writing the uppercase letter F on the lines below.

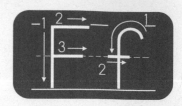

Practice writing the lowercase letter f on the lines below.

Write the words fox, foot, and friend on the lines below.

fox

foot

friend

Color the pictures that begin with the letter F.

Gg

Practice writing the uppercase letter G on the lines below.

Practice writing the lowercase letter g on the lines below.

Write the words great, golf, and gorilla on the lines below.

great _____   golf _____

gorilla _____

Circle the pictures that begin with the letter G.

Hh

Practice writing the uppercase letter H on the lines below.

Practice writing the lowercase letter h on the lines below.

Write the words happy, house, and hello on the lines below.

happy

house

hello

Draw three pictures that begin with the letter H.

Ii

Practice writing the uppercase letter I on the lines below.

Practice writing the lowercase letter i on the lines below.

Write the words icicle, island, and iguana on the lines below.

icicle   island

iguana

Color the pictures that begin with the letter I.

Jj

Practice writing the uppercase letter J on the lines below.

Practice writing the lowercase letter j on the lines below.

Write the words jug, jaw, and jump on the lines below.

jug

jaw

jump

Circle the pictures that begin with the letter J.

Kk

Practice writing the uppercase letter K on the lines below.

Practice writing the lowercase letter k on the lines below.

Write the words kind, kettle, and koala on the lines below.

kind

kettle

koala

Draw three pictures that begin with the letter K.

Ll

Practice writing the uppercase letter L on the lines below.

Practice writing the lowercase letter l on the lines below.

Write the words love, lamb, and light on the lines below.

love

lamb

light

Color the pictures that begin with the letter L.

Mm

Practice writing the uppercase letter M on the lines below.

M   M

Practice writing the lowercase letter m on the lines below.

m   m

Write the words me, mom, and muffin on the lines below.

me

mom

muffin

Circle the pictures that begin with the letter M.

Letter Formation

Nn

Practice writing the uppercase letter N on the lines below.

Practice writing the lowercase letter n on the lines below.

Write the words nest, nice, and numbers on the lines below.

nest

nice

numbers

Draw three pictures that begin with the letter N.

78

Oo

Practice writing the uppercase letter O on the lines below.

Practice writing the lowercase letter o on the lines below.

Write the words owl, one, and ostrich on the lines below.

owl

one

ostrich

Color the pictures that begin with the letter O.

Pp

Practice writing the uppercase letter P on the lines below.

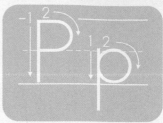

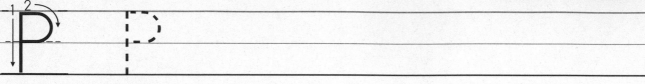

Practice writing the lowercase letter p on the lines below.

Write the words pig, pie, and people on the lines below.

pig

pie

people

Circle the pictures that begin with the letter P.

Qq

Practice writing the uppercase letter **Q** on the lines below.

Practice writing the lowercase letter **q** on the lines below.

Write the words queen, quilt, and quail on the lines below.

queen

quilt

quail

Draw three pictures that begin with the letter **Q**.

Rr

Practice writing the uppercase letter R on the lines below.

Practice writing the lowercase letter r on the lines below.

Write the words rain, rice, and rainbow on the lines below.

rain

rice

rainbow

Color the pictures that begin with the letter R.

Ss
Practice writing the uppercase letter S on the lines below.

S   S

Practice writing the lowercase letter s on the lines below.

s   s

Write the words sit, sink, and super on the lines below.

sit _____   sink _____

super _____

Circle the pictures that begin with the letter S.

Tt

Practice writing the uppercase letter T on the lines below.

Practice writing the lowercase letter t on the lines below.

Write the words tiger, table, and train on the lines below.

tiger

table

train

Draw three pictures that begin with the letter T.

Uu

Practice writing the uppercase letter U on the lines below.

Practice writing the lowercase letter u on the lines below.

Write the words up, under, and unicycle on the lines below.

up

under

unicycle

Color the pictures that begin with the letter U.

Vv

Practice writing the uppercase letter V on the lines below.

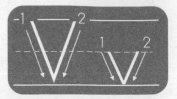

Practice writing the lowercase letter v on the lines below.

Write the words vest, vase, and violin on the lines below.

vest

vase

violin

Circle the pictures that begin with the letter V.

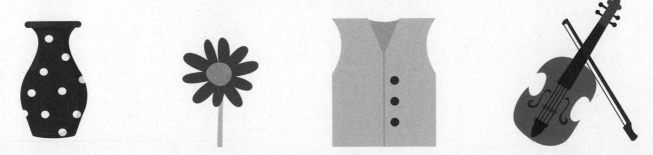

Ww

Practice writing the uppercase letter W on the lines below.

Practice writing the lowercase letter w on the lines below.

Write the words will, wood, and window on the lines below.

will

wood

window

Draw three pictures that begin with the letter W.

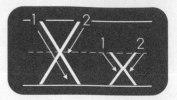

Xx

Practice writing the uppercase letter X on the lines below.

Practice writing the lowercase letter x on the lines below.

Write the words x-ray and xylophone on the lines below.

x-ray

xylophone

Color the pictures that begin with the letter X.

Yy

Practice writing the uppercase letter Y on the lines below.

Practice writing the lowercase letter y on the lines below.

Write the words yo-yo, yawn, and yellow on the lines below.

yo-yo _____   yawn _____

yellow _____

Circle the pictures that begin with the letter Y.

Zz

Practice writing the uppercase letter Z on the lines below.

Practice writing the lowercase letter z on the lines below.

Write the words zebra, zero, and zigzag on the lines below.

zebra _____ zero _____

zigzag _____

Draw three pictures that begin with the letter Z.

ABC Order

Some of the letters are missing!

Write the missing letters of the alphabet. Then color the mittens.

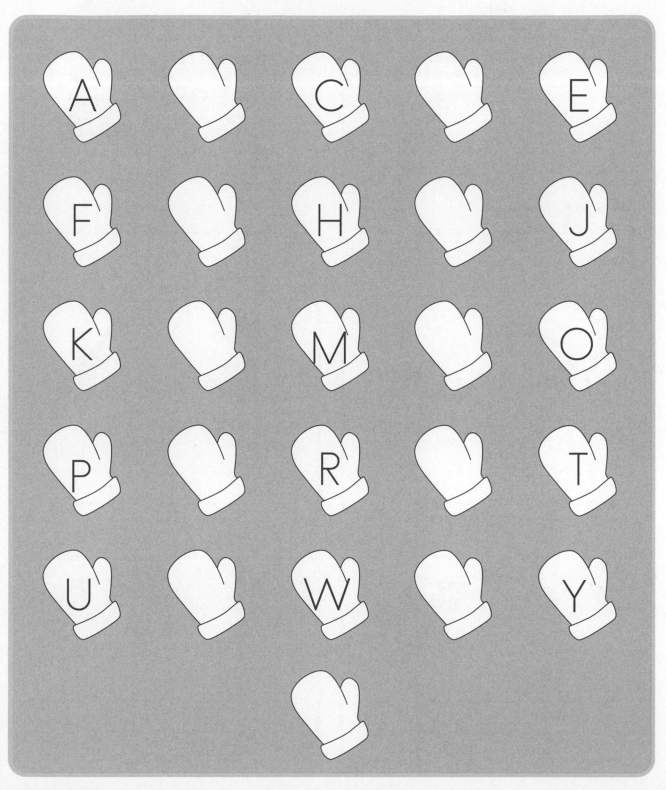

ABC Order

Sometimes we are asked to put words in alphabetical order. This means to put the words in the order of the ABCs.

Look at the first letter of each word. Which word comes first in ABC order? Write the word on the lines below.

snake   zebra

_____

_____

tiger   apple

_____

_____

monkey   caterpillar

_____

_____

koala   violin

_____

_____

umbrella   quilt

_____

_____

ice cream   juice

_____

_____

Singular or Plural?

Words look different when you are talking about one of something or more than one. Singular means one. Plural means more than one. When there is more than one person, place, or thing, most of the time an -s is added.

Decide if the words below are singular (one thing) or plural (two or more things). Write each word on the correct lines.

shoes

bee

porcupine

monkeys

frogs

zebra

insects

whale

Singular	Plural

93

Contractions

Contractions are two words made into one word.
An apostrophe is placed where some of the letters are removed.

Example: cannot becomes can't

Draw a line from the two words to their matching contraction.

did not	isn't
was not	didn't
is not	wasn't
have not	haven't

I have	you've
you have	I've
they have	we've
we have	they've

Contractions

Draw a line from the words to the correct contractions.

I will	you'll
you will	I'll
they will	she'll
she will	they'll

I am	she's
he is	I'm
she is	who's
it is	it's
who is	he's

Sentences

Every sentence starts with a capital letter and ends with a punctuation mark. Statement sentences tell the reader something. They start with a capital letter and end with a period.

This is a period .

Something is missing! Read the statement sentences and correct them on the lines below. Start with a capital letter and end with a period.

i like to read

you are my friend

the glass is full

that dog is brown

i see a bird

Sentences

Question sentences ask someone something. They start with a capital letter and end with a question mark.

This is a question mark ?

Something is missing! Read the question sentences and correct them on the lines below. Start with a capital letter and end with a question mark.

can you play with me

_____

_____

may I have a juice box

_____

_____

do you like ice cream

_____

_____

how do you ride a bike

_____

_____

will you walk the dog

_____

_____

Sentences

Exclamation sentences either tell someone to do something or express excitement. They start with a capital letter and end with an exclamation mark.

This is an exclamation mark !

Something is missing! Read the exclamation sentences and correct them on the lines below. Start with a capital letter and end with an exclamation mark.

look up at the bird

_____

_____

hooray, we won

_____

_____

ouch, that hurts

_____

_____

i found my shoes

_____

_____

i can help

_____

_____

Edit the Sentences

Look at the sentences below. There is something missing.

Read the sentences and write the proper punctuation at the end. Use a . , ?, or !

I went to the beach with my family __

Yay! We are going to the pool today __

Do you like to eat ice cream __

Look, Mom, my tooth came out __

I can play the piano __

Will you come and play with me __

Write a statement sentence about a pet.
_____
_____
_____

Write a question sentence about dessert.
_____
_____
_____

Write an exclamation sentence about something you are excited about.
_____
_____
_____

Fix the Sentences

Look at the sentences below. There is something missing.

Read the sentences and circle the mistakes in red. Then rewrite the sentences below with capital letters and the correct punctuation.

Example: It is time for bed.   It is time for bed.

i can brush my teeth

let's go to the park

ouch, I hurt my finger

do you have a pet

how fast can you run

you are my best friend

Nouns

Nouns are words for people, animals, places, and things.

Color the nouns in the gumball machine using the key. Then color the rest of the picture.

person = red   animal = blue

place = yellow   thing = green

Verbs

Verbs are words that tell what a noun is doing. They are action words.

Circle the verb in each sentence. Color the pictures.

That girl is (waving).

The boy ran to the park.

My teacher reads a book.

Your mom baked a cake.

The dog chased the cat.

The bird flew away.

I can jump rope.

The bunny is hopping.

Adjectives

Adjectives describe something. They tell how something looks, feels, smells, tastes, or sounds.

Read the words in each row. Circle the two words that describe the picture.

	green	hot	slippery	dirty
	fluffy	white	black	smelly
	cold	bright	purple	hot

Write an adjective to describe each picture.

Puppies are _____

Ice pops are _____

Rain is _____

Fire is _____

Brainstorming Lists

Authors write about things they know. Making a list of things they know about helps authors get ideas.

Write a list of things you know about on the lines below.

1. _____

2. _____

3. _____

4. _____

5. _____

6. _____

7. _____

8. _____

9. _____

10. _____

Brainstorming for Writing

Brainstorming Lists

Authors write about things they like. Making a list of things they like helps authors get ideas.

Write a list of things you like on the lines below.

1. _____

2. _____

3. _____

4. _____

5. _____

6. _____

7. _____

8. _____

9. _____

10. _____

Writing with Sentence Starters

Sentence starters can help give you ideas for writing.

Read the sentence starters and complete the sentence with your own thoughts.

My favorite place to go is...

_____

_____

_____

The best day ever was...

_____

_____

_____

When I grow up I want to...

_____

_____

_____

If I could be any animal, I would be...

_____

_____

_____

If I were a superhero, I would...

_____

_____

_____

Descriptive Writing

Descriptive Writing

Using adjectives to describe the things you write about makes your writing more interesting.

Add adjectives to complete the sentences below. Draw pictures to illustrate your sentences.

My _____ parrot can talk.

I can fly high into the _____ clouds.

We went to the beach on a _____ day.

My pet frog likes _____ lily pads.

Story Writing

Let's Write a Story!

A story has a beginning, middle, and end. Look at the picture. Write a sentence for what happens first. Write a sentence for what happens second. Then write a sentence for what happens last.

_____

_____

_____

_____

_____

_____

_____

_____

_____

_____

Story Writing

Let's Write a Story!

A good story has a beginning, middle, and end. When we write, it is important to put things in order.

Write a story about a real or make-believe birthday party. Tell what happens first, next, and last on the lines below.

First _____

_____

_____

Next _____

_____

_____

Last _____

_____

_____

Draw a picture to match your story.

Letter Writing

Writing a letter to a friend or a parent can be fun! Practice writing a letter below. Who will you be sending it to?

Fill in the missing parts of the letter on the lines below.

_____
_____
_____
Date

_____
_____

Dear _____,

Greeting—the name of the person you are writing to

_____
_____
_____
_____
_____
_____
_____
_____

Body—what you want to say to the person you are writing to

_____
_____
_____,

Closing—"Love" or "Your friend"

_____
_____
_____

Signature—your name

Letter Writing

Writing a letter can also be a nice way to say thank you.

Fill in the missing parts of the letter on the lines below.

_____

_____

_____

Date

_____

_____

Dear _____,

Greeting

_____

_____

_____

_____

_____

_____

Body

_____

_____

_____,

Closing

_____

_____

_____

Signature

Thank You

111

How-To Writing

How-To Writing

When you are writing to describe how to do something, you write the steps you take to do it.

On the lines below, write in order the four steps it takes to brush your teeth. Draw a picture to show each step.

1. _____

2. _____

3. _____

4. _____

How-To Writing

Choose something you know how to do.

On the lines below, write the steps you take in the order you do them. Draw a picture to show each step of the activity.

1. _____
   _____
   _____

2. _____
   _____
   _____

3. _____
   _____

4. _____
   _____

Comic Strip Writing

Speech Bubbles

It can be fun to write what characters are saying.

Look at the pictures. What do you think the characters are saying? In the speech bubbles below, write what they are saying.

Comic Strip Writing

Speech Bubbles

Look at the pictures. What do you think the characters are saying? In the speech bubbles below, write what they are saying.

Opinion Writing

Opinion writing is writing that explains the way you feel about a topic and the reasons you feel that way.

Example: My favorite flavor of ice cream is chocolate because it is sweet and yummy!

Write the name of your favorite animal on the lines below.

_____

I like _____

Write your reasons below.

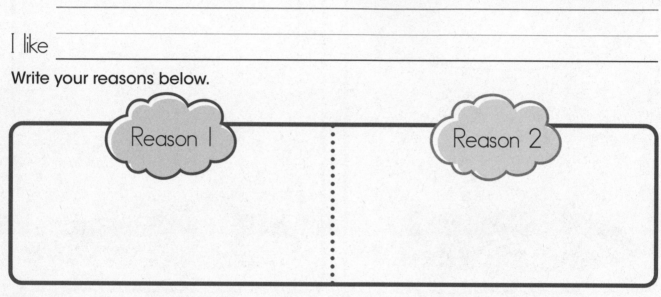

Rewrite your opinion with your reasons in a sentence on the lines below.

Draw a picture of your favorite animal.

Opinion Writing

Write the name of your favorite food on the lines below.

_____

I like _____

Write your reasons below.

Reason 1

Reason 2

Rewrite your opinion with your reasons in a sentence on the lines below.

_____
_____
_____
_____
_____
_____
_____

Draw a picture of your favorite food.

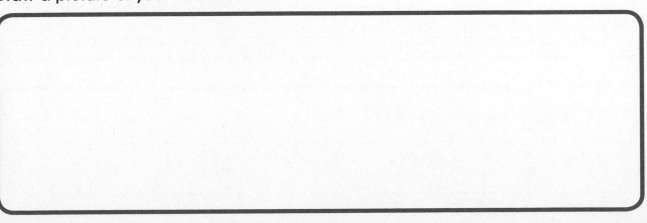

Graphic Organizers

Graphic Organizers

Graphic organizers are boxes and bubbles that help you put your thoughts in order before you write. Use the graphic organizer below to think about your writing.

Write in the boxes below to plan out your writing.

My favorite toy is
_____
_____
_____

Where did you get it?
_____
_____
_____

What does it look like?
_____
_____
_____

What do you do with it?
_____
_____
_____

How does it make you feel?
_____
_____
_____

Graphic Organizers

Write in the bubbles below to plan out your opinion writing.

Journal Writing

Journal Writing

Journal writing is like talking to a friend. It is about reflecting on what happens in your life and how you feel about what took place. You can draw in your journal, too!

Example: Yesterday I went to the park to play. It was really fun. I got to see my friends Maddy, Lucy, and Kate. I love playing at the park with my friends.

On the lines below, write about what you did yesterday and how the events made you feel.

_____

_____

_____

_____

_____

_____

_____

_____

_____

_____

_____

_____

Draw a picture of what you wrote about.

[ ]

Journal Writing

Journal Writing

Writing in a journal can also be about reflecting on what is going to happen in your life and how you feel about it. On the lines below, write about something you are looking forward to and how you feel about it.

_____

_____

_____

_____

_____

_____

_____

_____

_____

_____

Draw a picture of what you wrote about.

Creative Writing

Let's Write!

Write about anything you want on the lines below. Don't forget capital letters and punctuation! Need ideas? Look back at your lists of things you know a lot about and things you like.

Draw a picture of what you wrote about.

Let's Write!

Write about anything you want on the lines below. Don't forget capital letters and punctuation! Need ideas? Look back at your lists of things you know a lot about and things you like.

_____

_____

_____

_____

_____

_____

_____

_____

_____

_____

_____

_____

_____

Draw a picture of what you wrote about.

CERTIFICATE
of Achievement

....

has successfully completed
1st Grade Writing

Signed:

Date:

1²3 Math

Table of Contents

First Grade Math Readiness

Parents and caregivers are a child's first and most important teachers. Help your child be successful by talking about math in his or her daily life. Choose games and activities that incorporate adding and subtracting. Talk about things like how long until dinnertime or soccer practice. Teach them that math is important and fun!

Vocabulary Builder

Plus   + the word and symbol for adding

Minus   – the word and symbol for subtracting

Greater than   >

Less than   <

Equals   =

Writing Numbers 1-10

Trace and then practice writing the numbers on the lines below.

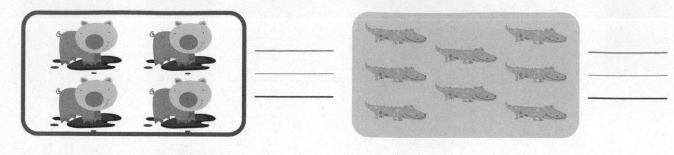

Counting 1-10

Count the pictures in each box and write the total number on the lines below.

 _____

 _____

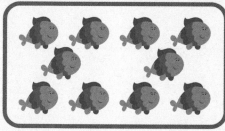 _____

 _____

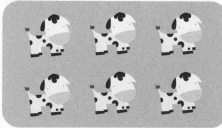 _____

 _____

 _____

 _____

 _____

 _____

 _____

 _____

 _____

 _____

 _____

Writing Numbers 11-20

Trace and then practice writing the numbers on the lines below.

Counting 11-20

Count the pictures in each box and write the total number on the lines below.

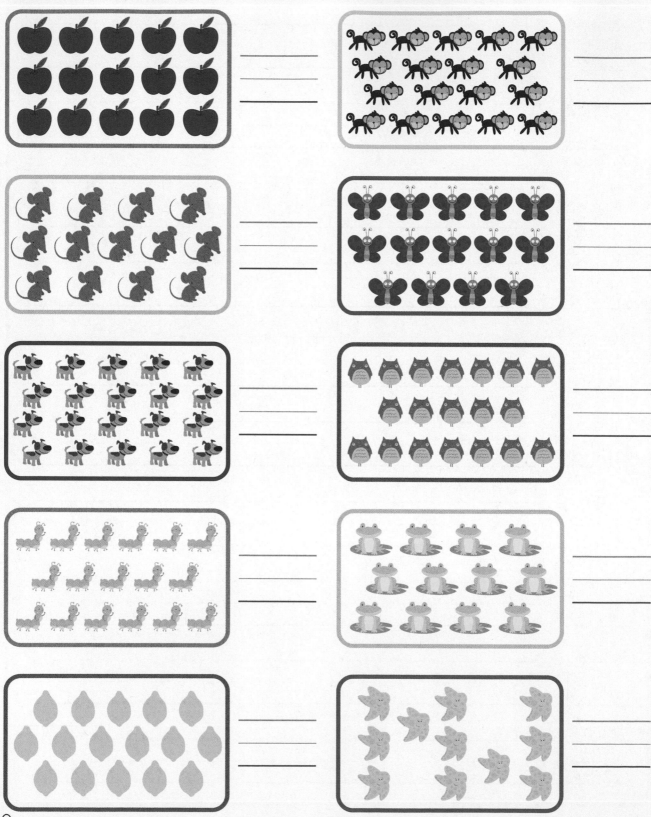

Number Words

Draw a line from the number word to the matching number.

one	3
two	4
three	1
four	2
five	7
six	5
seven	8
eight	6
nine	10
ten	9

Number Sense

Count to 50

Write the missing numbers on the snake.

Color it in when you're finished.

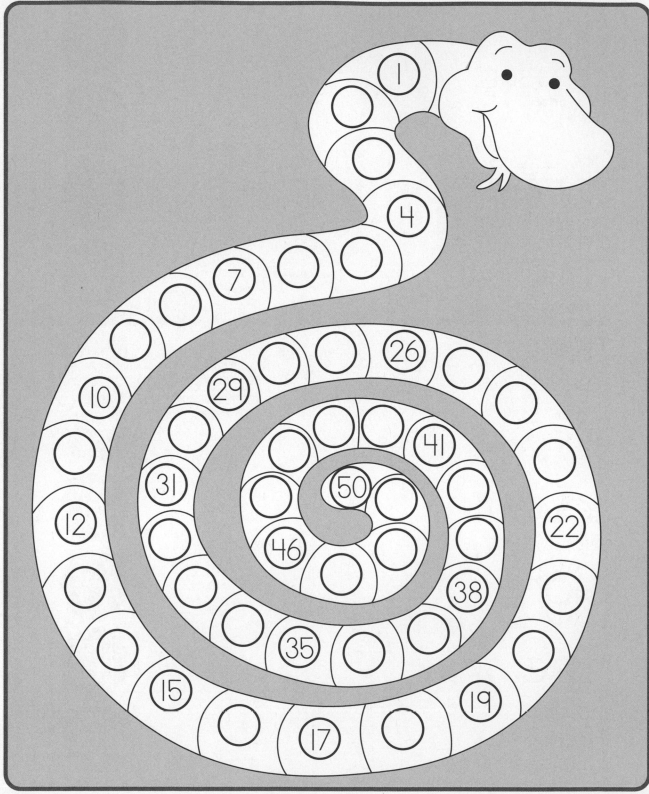

Counting 51-100

Connect the dots from 51 to 100.

Color your new friend when you're finished.

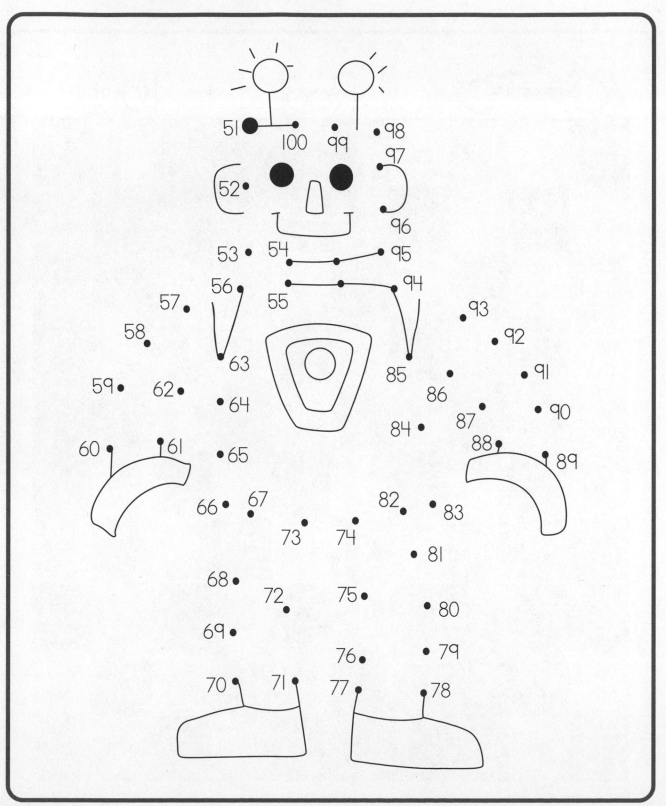

Race to 100

Write the missing numbers in each square to reach 100.

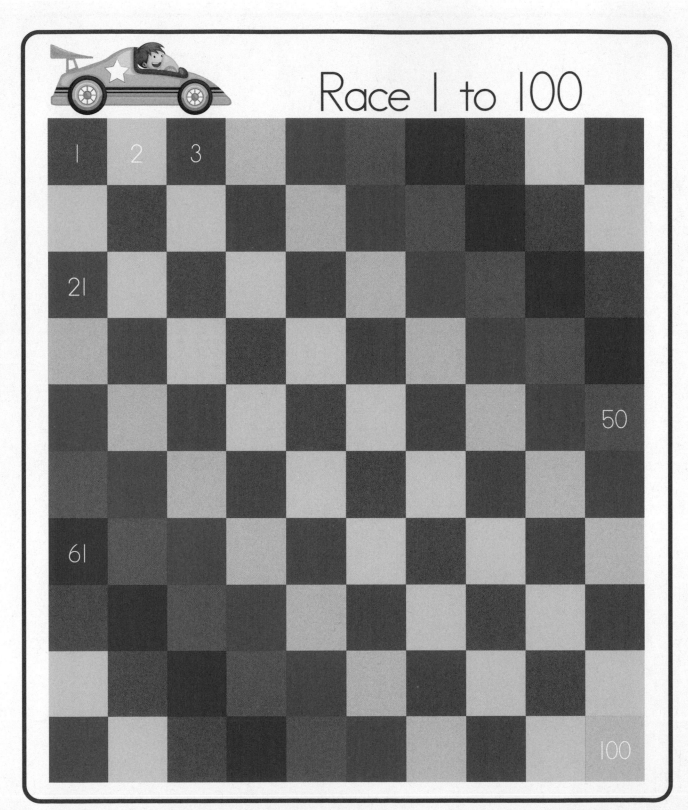

Race 1 to 100

1	2	3							
21									
								50
61									
								100

Count by Twos

Skip counting can make counting faster! Skip counting means skipping numbers as you count.

Circle groups of 2 objects while you skip count the pictures in each row. Write the number on the lines for how many you counted in each row.

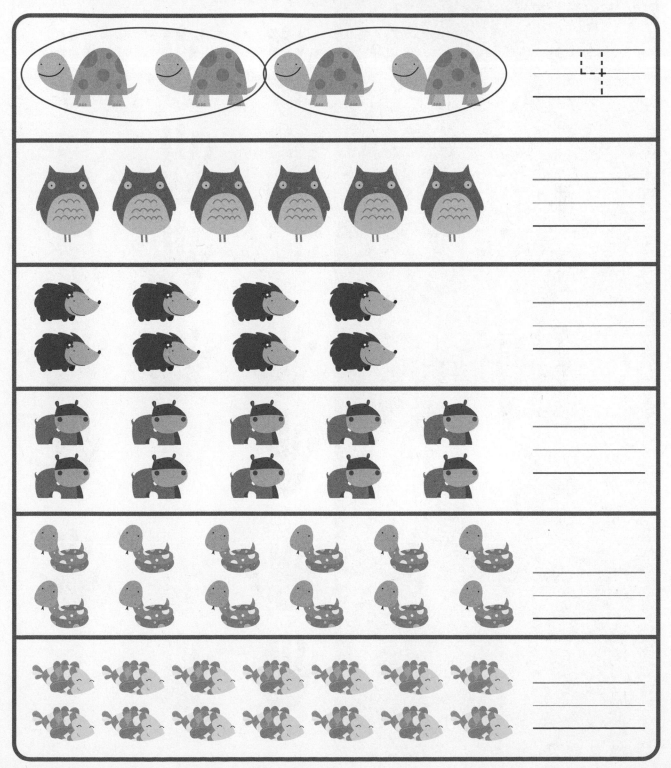

Count by Fives

Skip count by 5 up to 100 and write the missing numbers on the hands below.

Number Sense

Count by Tens

Count 10 objects at a time. Circle sets of 10 objects while you skip count the objects in each row. Write the number on the lines for how many you counted in each row.

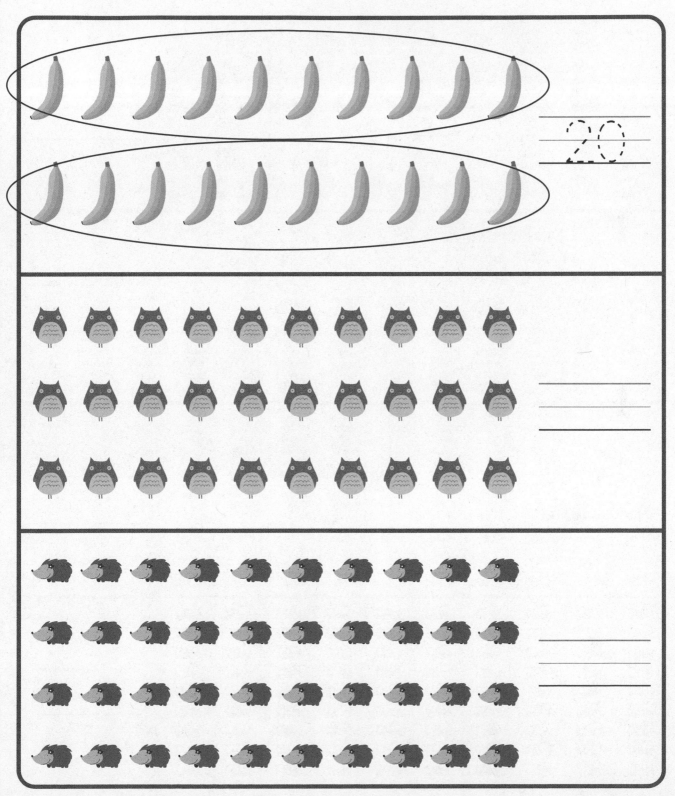

Number Sense

Count by Tens

Count 10 objects at a time. Circle sets of 10 objects while you skip count the pictures in each row. Write the number on the lines for how many you counted in each row.

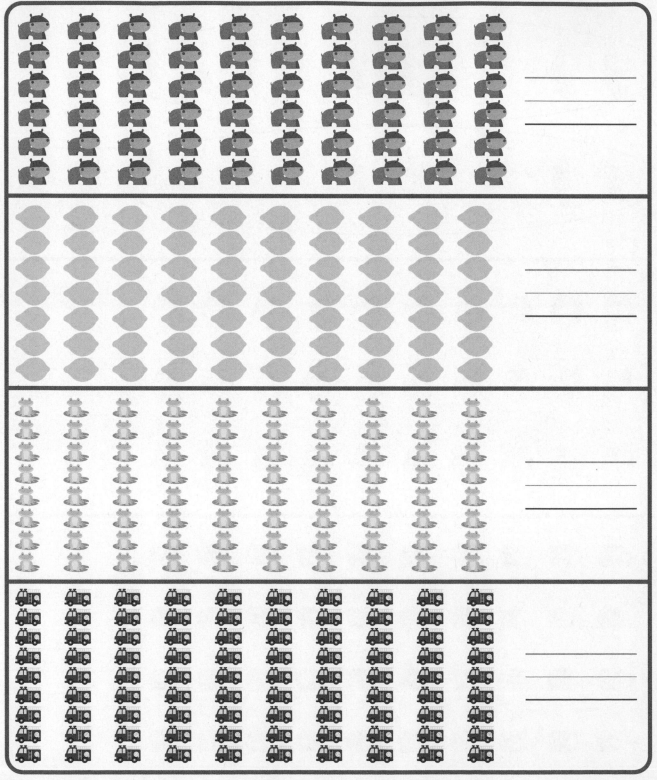

Addition

Practice Addition

Count the objects in each box and write the numbers in the equations. Write the sum after the equals sign.

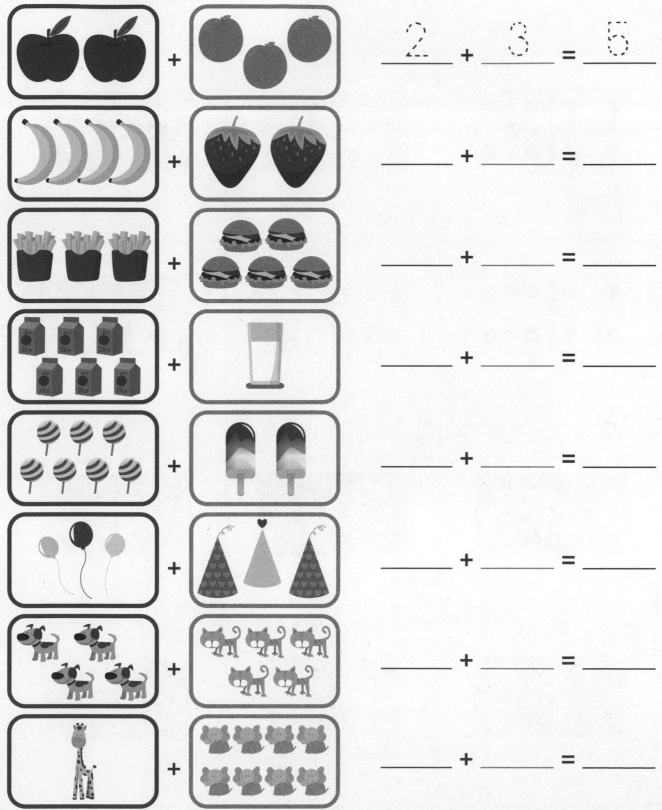

2 + 3 = 5

_____ + _____ = _____

_____ + _____ = _____

_____ + _____ = _____

_____ + _____ = _____

_____ + _____ = _____

_____ + _____ = _____

_____ + _____ = _____

Let's Play Dominoes!

Count the dots in each side of the domino and write the numbers in the equations. Write the sum after the equals sign.

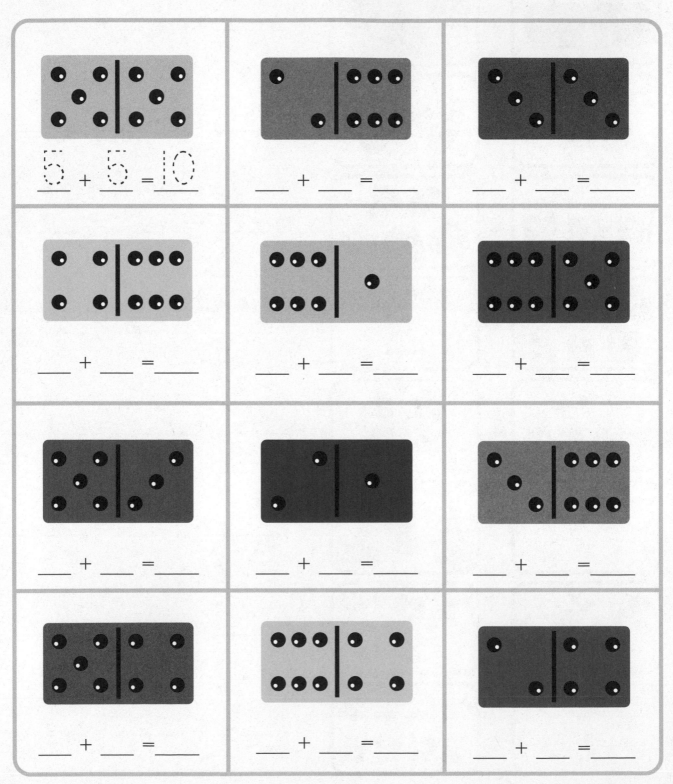

5 + 5 = 10

___ + ___ = ___

___ + ___ = ___

___ + ___ = ___

___ + ___ = ___

___ + ___ = ___

___ + ___ = ___

___ + ___ = ___

___ + ___ = ___

___ + ___ = ___

___ + ___ = ___

___ + ___ = ___

Addition

Vertical Equations

Count the red and green apples for each addition equation. Write the sum below each equals line.

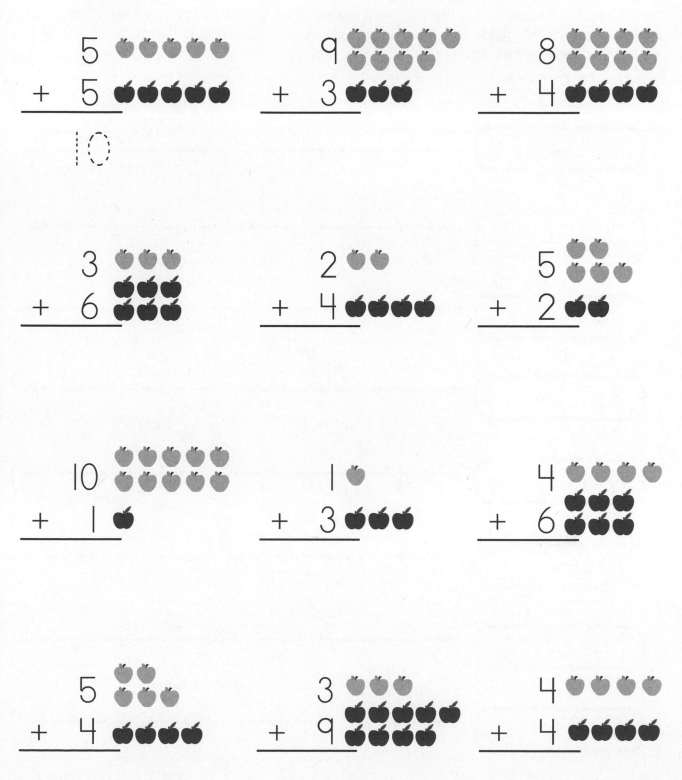

$$5 + 5 = 10$$

$$9 + 3 =$$

$$8 + 4 =$$

$$3 + 6 =$$

$$2 + 4 =$$

$$5 + 2 =$$

$$10 + 1 =$$

$$1 + 3 =$$

$$4 + 6 =$$

$$5 + 4 =$$

$$3 + 9 =$$

$$4 + 4 =$$

Using a Number Line

You can use a number line to help you count when adding.

Start on the number line at the first number in the equation. Then jump forward the number of spaces for the amount being added to the first number. Circle the number on the number line where the jump line ends. This is the sum. Write the sum after the equals sign.

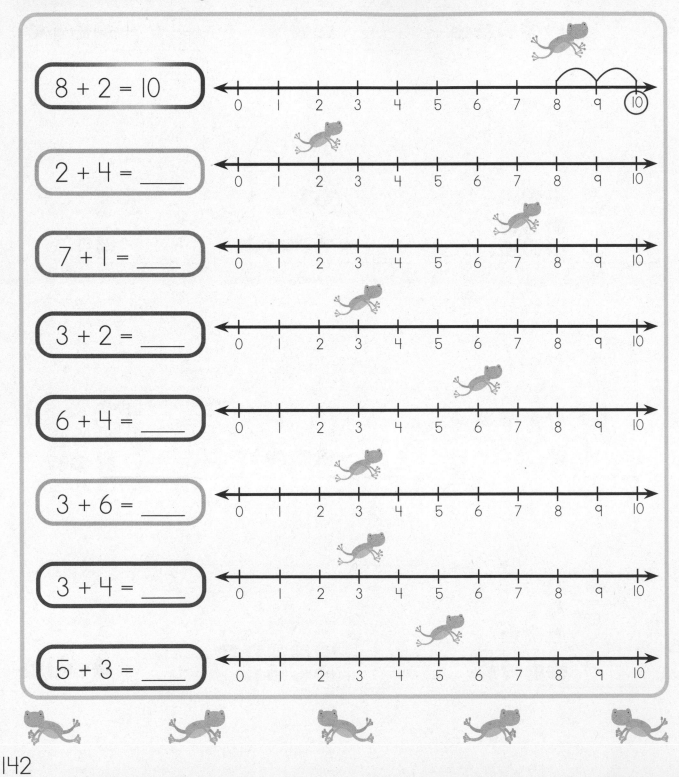

$8 + 2 = 10$

$2 + 4 = \underline{\quad}$

$7 + 1 = \underline{\quad}$

$3 + 2 = \underline{\quad}$

$6 + 4 = \underline{\quad}$

$3 + 6 = \underline{\quad}$

$3 + 4 = \underline{\quad}$

$5 + 3 = \underline{\quad}$

Addition

Using a Number Line

Start on the first number in the equation. Then jump forward on the line the same number of spaces as the second number. Draw a line from the first number to the second number and circle the correct answer. Then write the answers to the equations on the lines below.

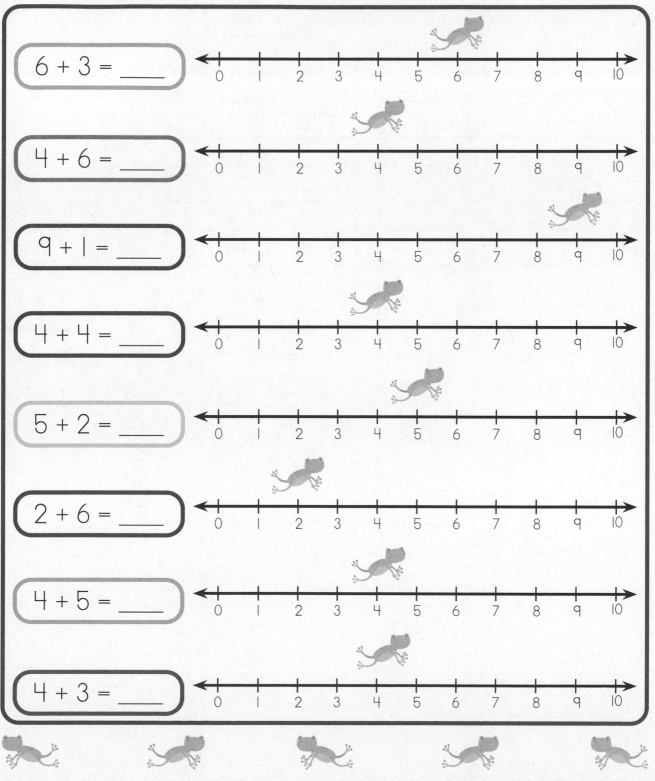

6 + 3 = ___

4 + 6 = ___

9 + 1 = ___

4 + 4 = ___

5 + 2 = ___

2 + 6 = ___

4 + 5 = ___

4 + 3 = ___

Sunny Summer Math

Solve the addition equations and write the sums on the lines below. Then color the pictures.

4 + 8 = ___

4 + 6 = ___

5 + 6 = ___

9 + 3 = ___

6 + 6 = ___

5 + 7 = ___

9 + 1 = ___

5 + 1 = ___

8 + 3 = ___

7 + 5 = ___

9 + 2 = ___

7 + 4 = ___

6 + 2 = ___

1 + 6 = ___

6 + 3 = ___

10 + 2 = ___

11 + 1 = ___

4 + 4 = ___

8 + 5 = ___

3 + 8 = ___

Word Problems

Sometimes math equations are hidden in story problems. Read each addition story problem carefully and figure out the unknown number to solve the equation. Write that number on the line in each equation.

Example: Maddy has ②red beads. She got ③more beads from a friend. How many beads does Maddy have now?

$$2 + 3 = \underline{5}$$

Circle the clues and solve the word problems. Write your answers on the lines below.

1. Lucy has a seashell collection. She was given 3 more seashells. Now she has 10 seashells. How many seashells did she have before she got some more?

$$\underline{\quad} + 3 = 10$$

2. Emma invites 10 children to her party. Some girls and 5 boys came. How many girls were invited?

$$5 + \underline{\quad} = 10$$

3. Sophia likes to run. She runs 4 miles on Monday and 6 miles on Tuesday. How far did she run in two days?

$$4 + 6 = \underline{\quad}$$

4. Noah has 2 toy trucks. Luke has 7 toy trucks. How many more toy trucks does Luke have than Noah?

$$2 + \underline{\quad} = 7$$

Add to the Fun

Solve the addition problems. Write the answers below.

2 + 0	3 + 1	2 + 6	3 + 3	2 + 5
7 + 1	6 + 3	1 + 9	5 + 6	10 + 2
5 + 7	3 + 8	4 + 5	0 + 7	5 + 4
8 + 4	3 + 7			
7 + 5	5 + 5			
0 + 9	4 + 1			

Addition

Word Problems

Read each addition story problem carefully and figure out the unknown number to solve the equation. Write that number on the line in each equation.

1. Sarah has 5 test tubes. She has 3 yellow and the rest are red. How many test tubes are red?

$$3 + \underline{} = 5$$

2. Lauren has 4 T-shirts with a red heart on them. She has 5 T-shirts with a dog on them. How many T-shirts does she own?

$$4 + 5 = \underline{}$$

3. Ashley has 8 shoes. She has 6 shoes with laces and the rest have buttons. How many shoes have buttons?

$$6 + \underline{} = 8$$

4. Kim painted her nails. She has 3 fewer pink nails than blue nails on her hands. How many blue nails does she have?

$$\underline{} + 3 = 10$$

Counting Backward

Counting backward helps you learn how to subtract numbers. Count backward by 1s and write the missing numbers in each caterpillar sequence as you count. Then color the caterpillars.

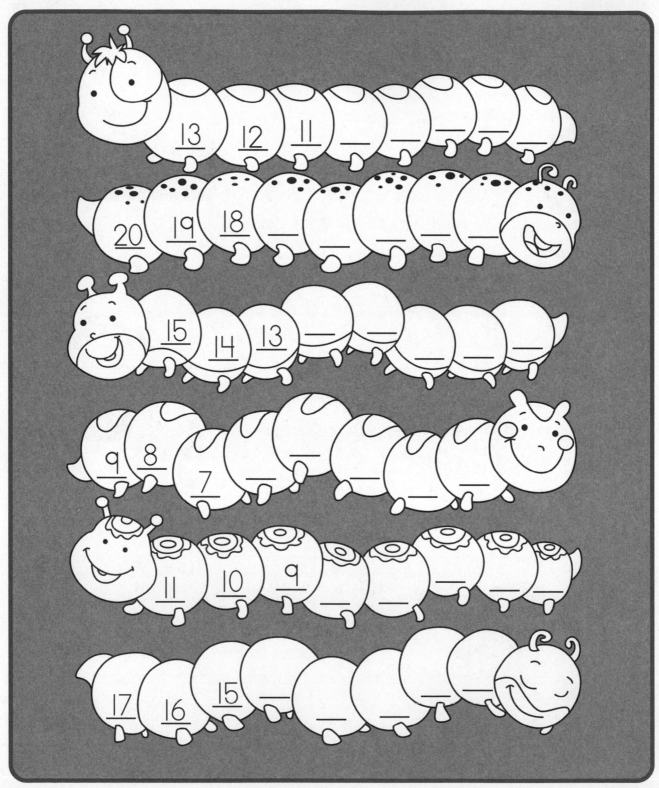

Subtraction

Practice Subtraction

Subtracting is taking away part of a whole number.

When we use pictures to subtract, we start with the whole number and then cross out the number of objects we are subtracting.

Example: $6 - 2 = 4$

Count the total number of objects in each row. Count backward for the amount of the second number in the equation which will be the x objects. The number of objects left is the difference. Write the difference under the equals line.

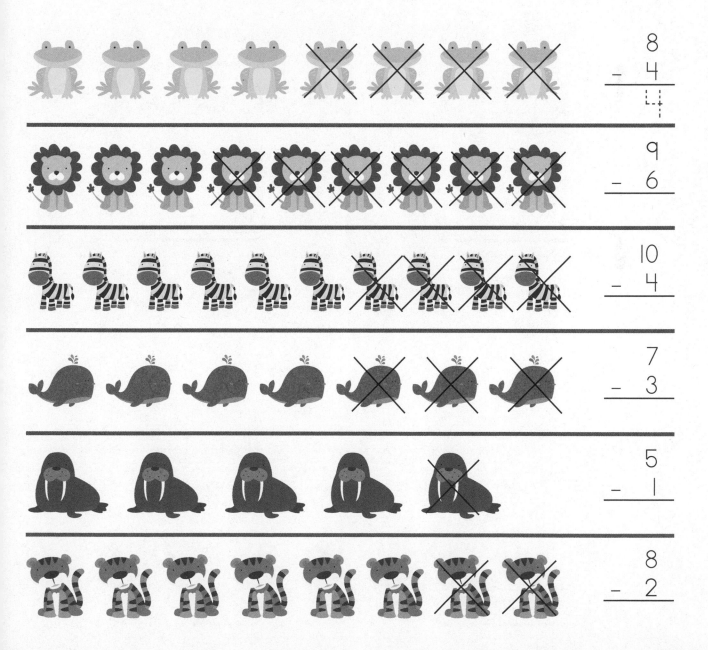

$$\begin{array}{r} 8 \\ -\ 4 \\ \hline 4 \end{array}$$

$$\begin{array}{r} 9 \\ -\ 6 \\ \hline \end{array}$$

$$\begin{array}{r} 10 \\ -\ 4 \\ \hline \end{array}$$

$$\begin{array}{r} 7 \\ -\ 3 \\ \hline \end{array}$$

$$\begin{array}{r} 5 \\ -\ 1 \\ \hline \end{array}$$

$$\begin{array}{r} 8 \\ -\ 2 \\ \hline \end{array}$$

Subtraction

Practice Subtraction

Cross out the number of objects you are subtracting from the total. Count the objects left and write the difference after the equals sign.

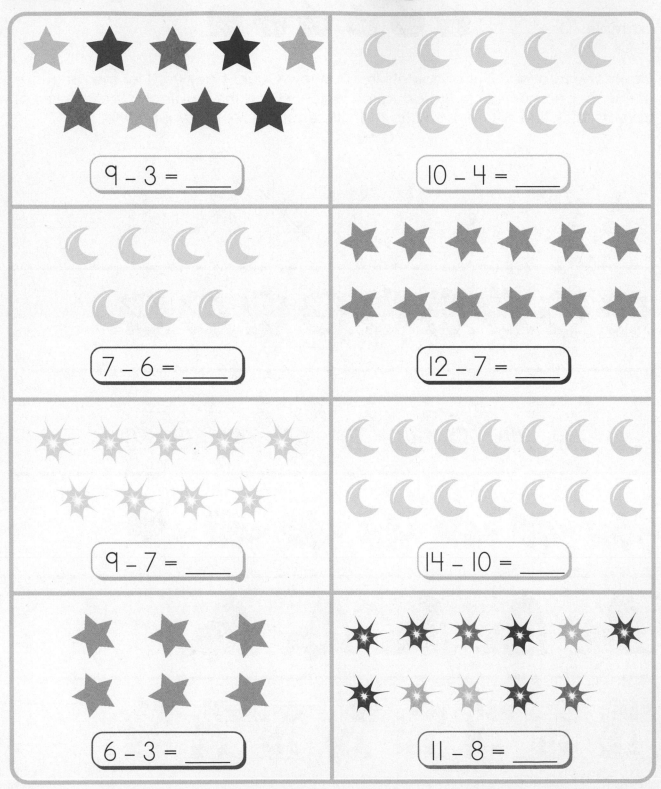

9 – 3 = ____

10 – 4 = ____

7 – 6 = ____

12 – 7 = ____

9 – 7 = ____

14 – 10 = ____

6 – 3 = ____

11 – 8 = ____

Subtraction

Practice Subtraction

Cross out the number of objects you are subtracting from the total. Count the objects left and write the difference after the equals sign.

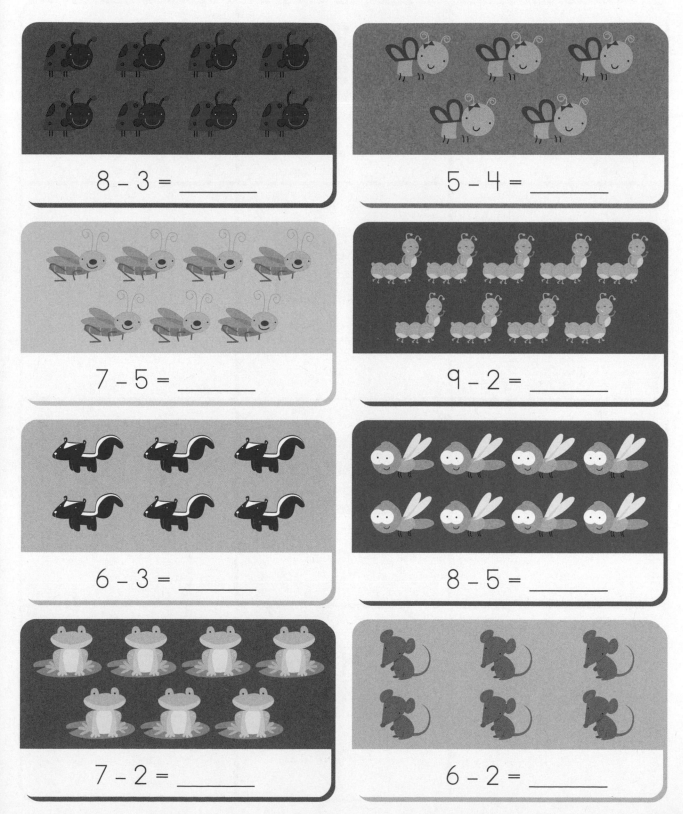

8 – 3 = _____

5 – 4 = _____

7 – 5 = _____

9 – 2 = _____

6 – 3 = _____

8 – 5 = _____

7 – 2 = _____

6 – 2 = _____

Let's Play Dominoes!

Use the dots on the dominoes to help you subtract. Write the difference for each equation after the equals sign.

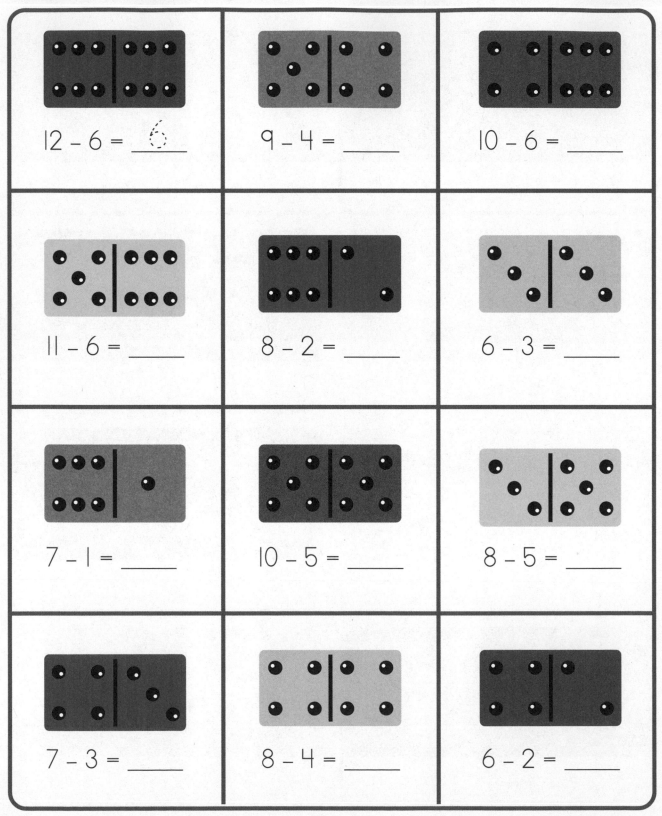

12 – 6 = 6

9 – 4 = _____

10 – 6 = _____

11 – 6 = _____

8 – 2 = _____

6 – 3 = _____

7 – 1 = _____

10 – 5 = _____

8 – 5 = _____

7 – 3 = _____

8 – 4 = _____

6 – 2 = _____

Subtraction

Word Problems

Sometimes math equations are hidden in story problems. Read each subtraction story problem carefully and figure out the unknown number to solve the equation. Write that number on the line in each equation.

Example: Maddy said there were ⑤ apples on the table. She ate some. Now there are ② apples. How many did Maddy eat?

5 - _3_ = 2

Circle the clues and solve the word problems. Write your answers on the lines below.

1. Juan has 5 trading cards. He gave 2 away as gifts. How many does he still have?

5 - 2 = ___

2. Oliver popped 4 balloons at the party. Mason popped 8 balloons. How many fewer balloons did Oliver pop than Mason?

8 - 4 = ___

3. Logan has some drums on Monday. He gave 5 drums away on Tuesday. Now he has 4 drums. How many drums did he have on Monday?

___ - 5 = 4

4. Hannah has 4 fewer sheep than Riley. Riley has 7 sheep. How many sheep does Hannah have?

7 - 4 = ___

Subtraction

Using a Number Line

You can use a number line to help you count when subtracting.

Start on the number line at the first number in the equation. Then, jump backward the number of spaces for the amount being taken away from the first number. Circle the number on the number line where the jump line ends. This is the difference. Write the difference after the equals sign.

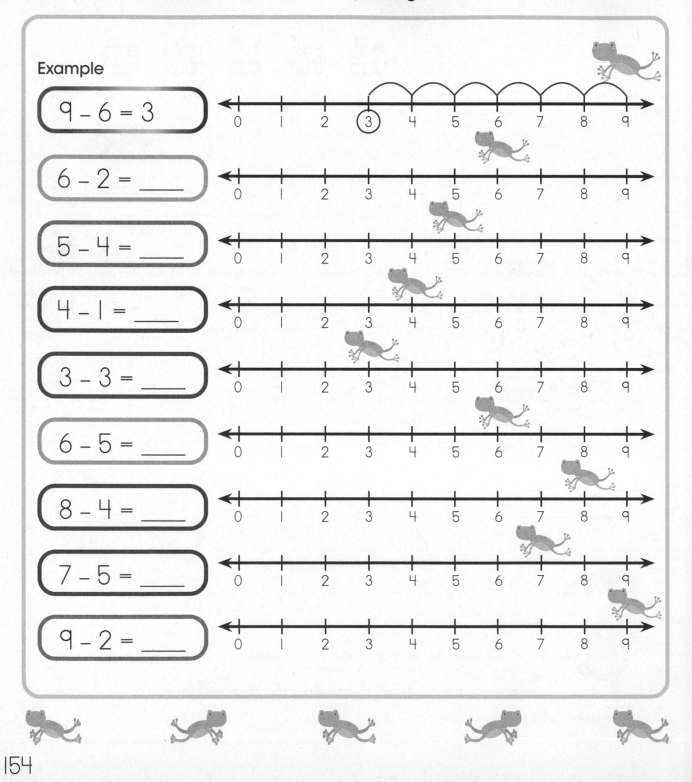

Example

$9 - 6 = 3$

$6 - 2 = \underline{}$

$5 - 4 = \underline{}$

$4 - 1 = \underline{}$

$3 - 3 = \underline{}$

$6 - 5 = \underline{}$

$8 - 4 = \underline{}$

$7 - 5 = \underline{}$

$9 - 2 = \underline{}$

Using a Number Line

Start on the number line at the first number in the equation. Then, jump backward the number of spaces for the amount being taken away from the first number. Circle the number on the number line where the jump line ends. This is the difference. Write the difference after the equals sign.

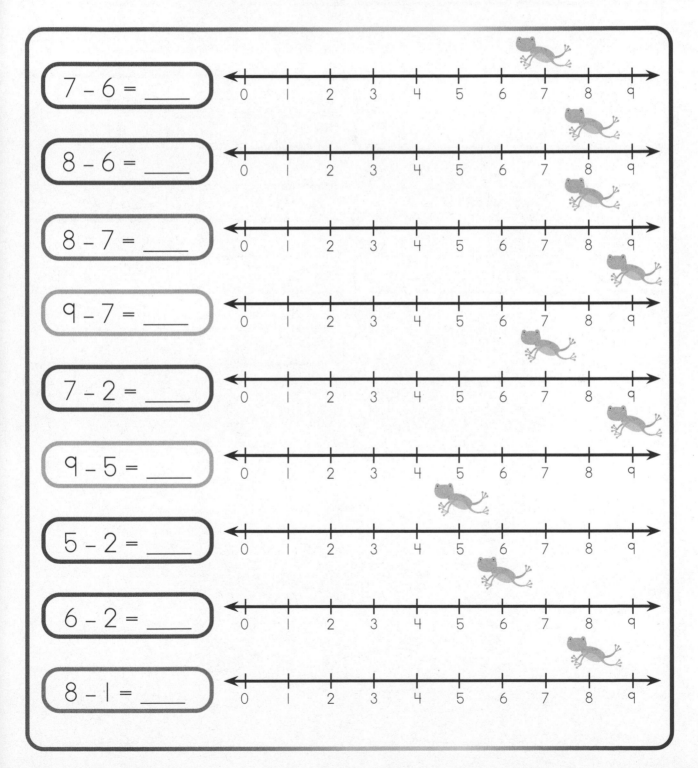

7 – 6 = ___

8 – 6 = ___

8 – 7 = ___

9 – 7 = ___

7 – 2 = ___

9 – 5 = ___

5 – 2 = ___

6 – 2 = ___

8 – 1 = ___

Math Can Be a Picnic!

Solve the subtraction equations and write the differences after the equals signs.

10 – 4 = _____   12 – 8 = _____   15 – 6 = _____   10 – 8 = _____

16 – 7 = _____   18 – 9 = _____   14 – 7 = _____   12 – 2 = _____

12 – 4 = _____   11 – 7 = _____   15 – 9 = _____   18 – 10 = _____

15 – 8 = _____   11 – 2 = _____   17 – 9 = _____   16 – 0 = _____

12 – 7 = _____   17 – 8 = _____   13 – 7 = _____   18 – 0 = _____

14 – 5 = _____   12 – 9 = _____   16 – 9 = _____   9 – 7 = _____

Word Problems

Read each subtraction story problem carefully and figure out the unknown number to solve the equation. Write that number on the line in each equation.

1. Avery has 10 students in her class. Some students went to the nurse. Now she has 3 students. How many children are not feeling well?

$$10 - \underline{\quad} = 3$$

2. Emily has 4 tomatoes. Lily has 8 tomatoes. How many fewer tomatoes does Emily have than Lily?

$$8 - 4 = \underline{\quad}$$

3. Connor has 9 tents. He has 3 brown tents and the rest are green. How many tents are green?

$$9 - 3 = \underline{\quad}$$

4. Trevor has some canoes for rent. He rents 2 out in the afternoon. Now he has 5 canoes. How many did he have in the morning?

$$\underline{\quad} - 2 = 5$$

Subtraction

Vertical Equations

Solve the subtraction equations. Write the differences below the equals lines.

BEACH

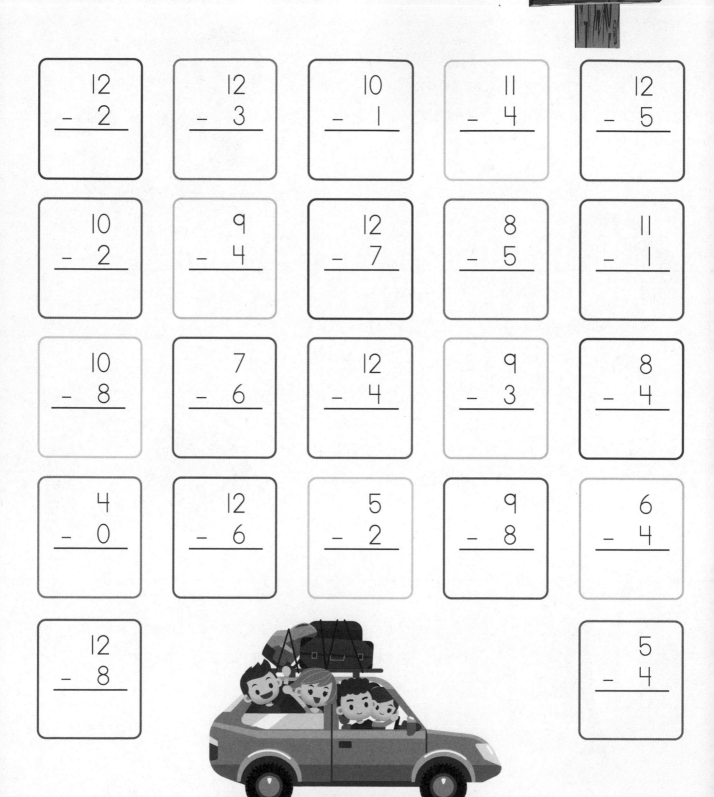

$$\begin{array}{r} 12 \\ -\ 2 \\ \hline \end{array}$$

$$\begin{array}{r} 12 \\ -\ 3 \\ \hline \end{array}$$

$$\begin{array}{r} 10 \\ -\ 1 \\ \hline \end{array}$$

$$\begin{array}{r} 11 \\ -\ 4 \\ \hline \end{array}$$

$$\begin{array}{r} 12 \\ -\ 5 \\ \hline \end{array}$$

$$\begin{array}{r} 10 \\ -\ 2 \\ \hline \end{array}$$

$$\begin{array}{r} 9 \\ -\ 4 \\ \hline \end{array}$$

$$\begin{array}{r} 12 \\ -\ 7 \\ \hline \end{array}$$

$$\begin{array}{r} 8 \\ -\ 5 \\ \hline \end{array}$$

$$\begin{array}{r} 11 \\ -\ 1 \\ \hline \end{array}$$

$$\begin{array}{r} 10 \\ -\ 8 \\ \hline \end{array}$$

$$\begin{array}{r} 7 \\ -\ 6 \\ \hline \end{array}$$

$$\begin{array}{r} 12 \\ -\ 4 \\ \hline \end{array}$$

$$\begin{array}{r} 9 \\ -\ 3 \\ \hline \end{array}$$

$$\begin{array}{r} 8 \\ -\ 4 \\ \hline \end{array}$$

$$\begin{array}{r} 4 \\ -\ 0 \\ \hline \end{array}$$

$$\begin{array}{r} 12 \\ -\ 6 \\ \hline \end{array}$$

$$\begin{array}{r} 5 \\ -\ 2 \\ \hline \end{array}$$

$$\begin{array}{r} 9 \\ -\ 8 \\ \hline \end{array}$$

$$\begin{array}{r} 6 \\ -\ 4 \\ \hline \end{array}$$

$$\begin{array}{r} 12 \\ -\ 8 \\ \hline \end{array}$$

$$\begin{array}{r} 5 \\ -\ 4 \\ \hline \end{array}$$

Comparing Numbers

Comparing numbers means deciding how the numbers are different and categorizing them as more or less.

If a number is more, we say it is greater than the other number. If a number is less, we say it is less than the other number.

Look at the two numbers in each box below. Which number is the greater amount? Circle the greater amount.

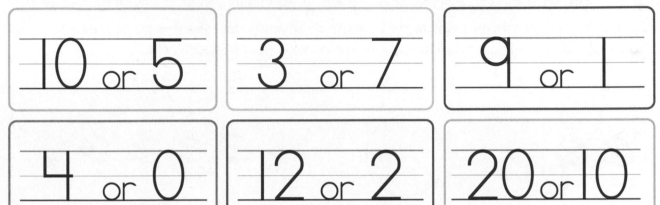

Look at the two numbers in each box below. Which number is the lesser amount? Circle the lesser amount.

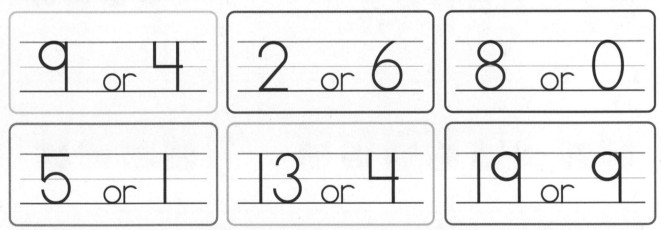

Comparing Numbers

Greater Than, Less Than, and Equal To

The symbol for greater than is >.

The symbol for less than is <.

The symbol for equal to is =.

Equal to means the same amount as.

Sometimes using the greater than > and less than < symbols can be confusing! Try to remember that the open end of both symbols will face the greater amount.

Compare the amounts of objects in each row. Write the greater than > or less than < symbol in the circle based on the amount on the left side.

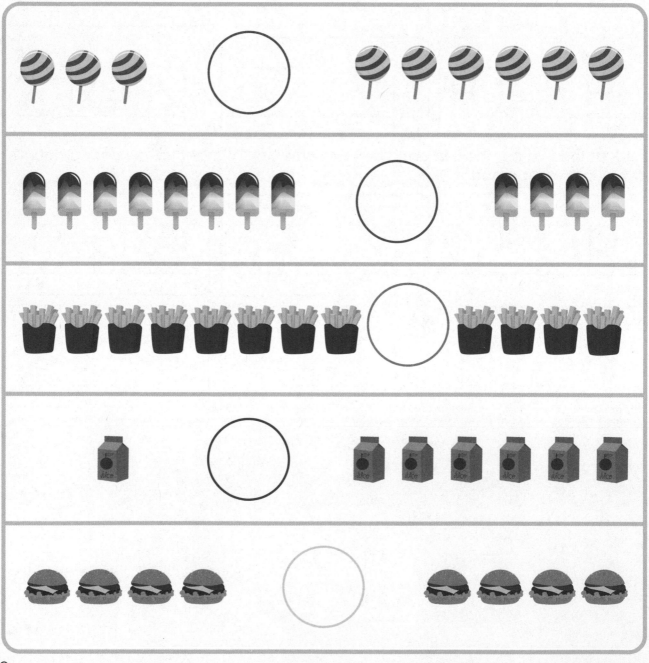

Equal Shares

Equal Shares

Equal shares are parts of a whole. Equal shares must have the same size parts.
Example:

equal   not equal

Color the shapes below that have equal shares.

2 equal shares means dividing a whole into two equal parts.

Each part is 1 out of 2 parts of the whole.

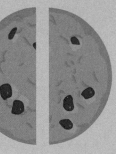

Color the shapes below:

1 out of 2 parts - red

1 out of 2 parts - yellow

 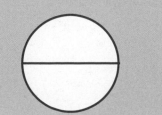

161

One Fourth

One fourth or $\frac{1}{4}$ means cutting a whole into four equal parts.
Each part is $\frac{1}{4}$ of the whole.

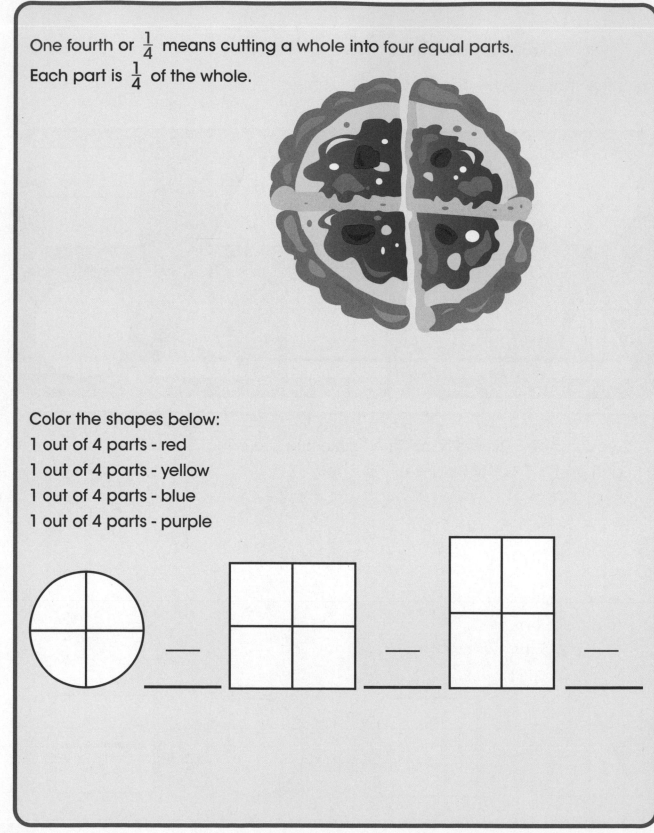

Color the shapes below:
1 out of 4 parts - red
1 out of 4 parts - yellow
1 out of 4 parts - blue
1 out of 4 parts - purple

Place Value

Tens and Ones

Numbers with 2 digits have tens and ones.

The place of each digit tells which one it is.

Example: 15 = 1 ten and 5 ones.

The picture of ten blocks represent 1 bundle of ten.

The picture of five blocks represent 5 individual ones.

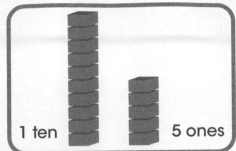

1 ten   5 ones

Look at the illustrations below and write how many tens and how many ones are in each group. Then, use those numbers to write the totals in the boxes.

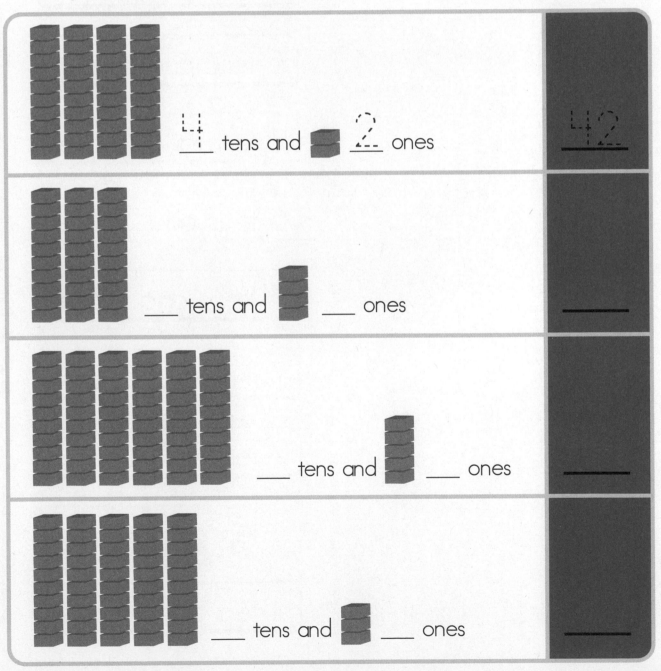

__4__ tens and __2__ ones   42

___ tens and ___ ones

___ tens and ___ ones

___ tens and ___ ones

Place Value

Tens and Ones
Draw a line from each number to the matching tens and ones.

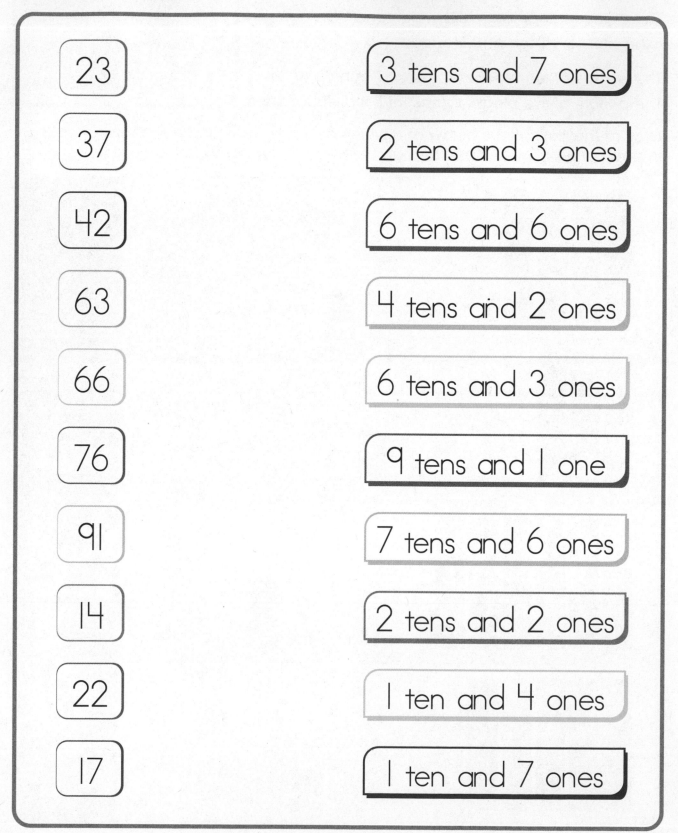

23	3 tens and 7 ones
37	2 tens and 3 ones
42	6 tens and 6 ones
63	4 tens and 2 ones
66	6 tens and 3 ones
76	9 tens and 1 one
91	7 tens and 6 ones
14	2 tens and 2 ones
22	1 ten and 4 ones
17	1 ten and 7 ones

Place Value

Tens and Ones

Write how many tens and ones are in each number on the lines below.

21 = ___ tens and ___ one

54 = ___ tens and ___ ones

15 = ___ ten and ___ ones

73 = ___ tens and ___ ones

24 = ___ tens and ___ ones

52 = ___ tens and ___ ones

42 = ___ tens and ___ ones

19 = ___ ten and ___ ones

81 = ___ tens and ___ one

11 = ___ ten and ___ one

66 = ___ tens and ___ ones

34 = ___ tens and ___ ones

53 = ___ tens and ___ ones

Length

We can measure the length of something in two ways.

We can use a nonstandard form of measurement, such as a paper clip or a stacking cube, or we can use a standard form of measurement, such as a ruler, which measures in inches.

Measure the items below with a nonstandard form of measurement and write the lengths on the lines below.

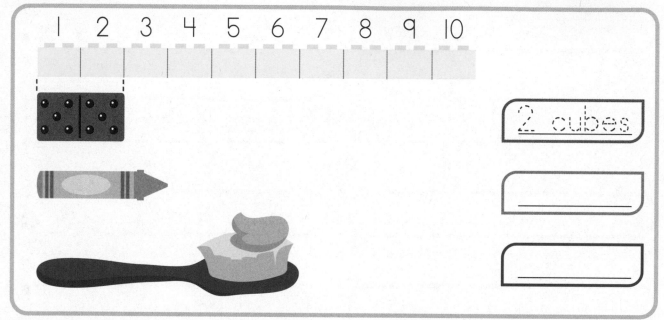

2 cubes

Measure the items below with a standard form of measurement and write the lengths on the lines below.

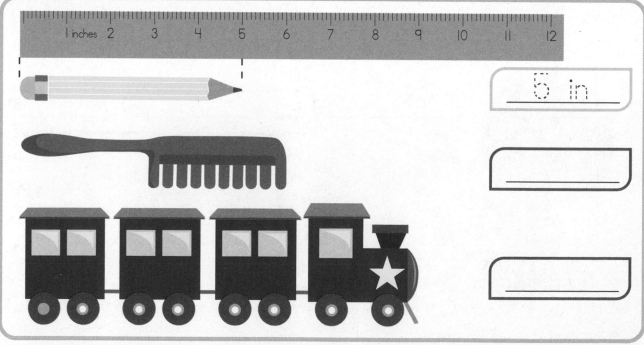

5 in

Longer and Shorter

Circle the objects that are longer. Cross out the objects that are shorter.

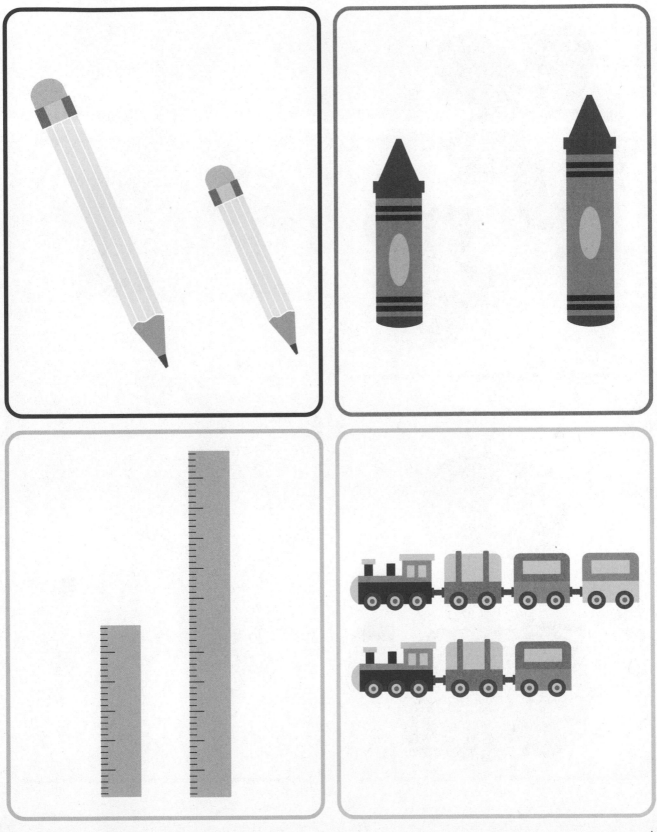

Measurement

Bigger and Smaller

Circle the objects that are bigger. Cross out the objects that are smaller.

Heavier and Lighter

Circle the objects that are heavier. Cross out the objects that are lighter.

Comparing Sizes

Compare the pictures below.

Circle the taller.

Circle the smaller.

Circle the heavier.

Circle the bigger.

Circle the shorter.

Circle the longer.

Capacity

Circle the objects below that hold more.

Cross out the objects that hold less.

Clocks and Telling Time

Clocks can look different.

This is an analog clock.

It has a long hand and a short hand.

It has the numbers 1-12 on its face.

The long hand points to the minute and the short hand points to the hour. This clock says 5 o'clock.

45 minutes after the hour (quarter to)

30 minutes after the hour (half past)

This is a digital clock.

The first number shows the hour, and the second two numbers tell how many minutes after the hour it is. This clock says 3 o'clock.

hour   minutes

Write the digital time under each analog clock.

7:00

Time to the Hour

Write the digital time under each analog clock.

What time is it? Draw two hands on each clock to match the digital time.

Time to the Half Hour

Write the digital time under each analog clock.

1:30

What time is it? Draw two hands on each analog clock to match the digital time.

2:30

4:30

6:30

8:00

10:00

12:30

Time to the Hour and Half Hour

Draw a line to match the digital time to the analog clock.

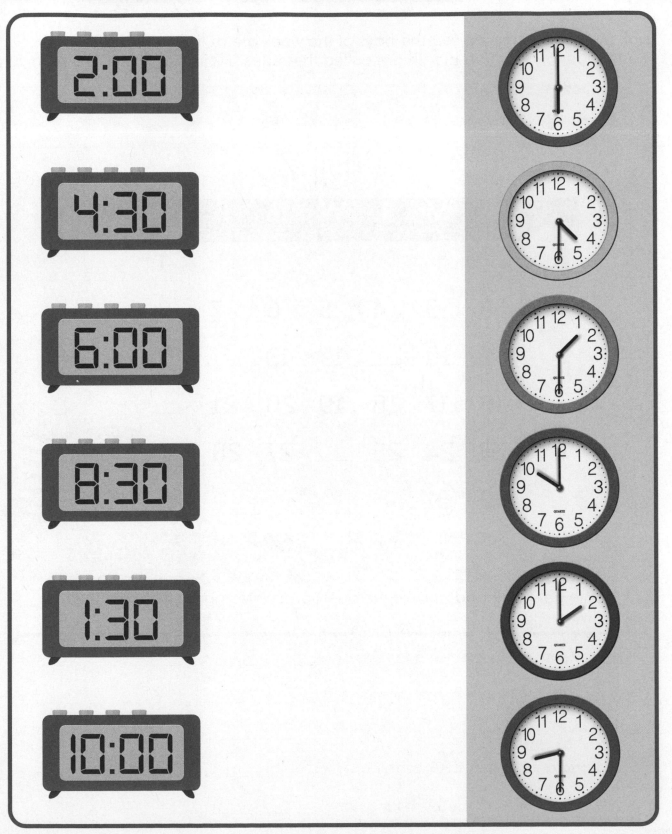

Calendars

There are 12 months in a year. April, June, September, and November all have 30 days. The other months have 31 days, except February. It is the shortest month with just 28 days.

Look at the calendar below. The days of the week are at the top of the month. The number of days in a month are called the dates. Fill in the missing dates in July.

Look at the calendar and answer the questions. Write your answers on the lines below.

Which month does this calendar show? _____

How many Fridays are in the month? _____

How many Saturdays are in the month? _____

How many days are in this month? _____

What is the date of the birthday party? _____

Geometry

3-Dimensional Shapes

3-D shapes are solid, not flat.
A sphere is like a bouncy ball.
A cube is like dice you roll.
A prism is like a tall building.
A cylinder is like a can of soda.
A cone is like a party hat.
3-D shapes are here and there.
3-D shapes are everywhere!

Color the 3-D shapes using the key below.

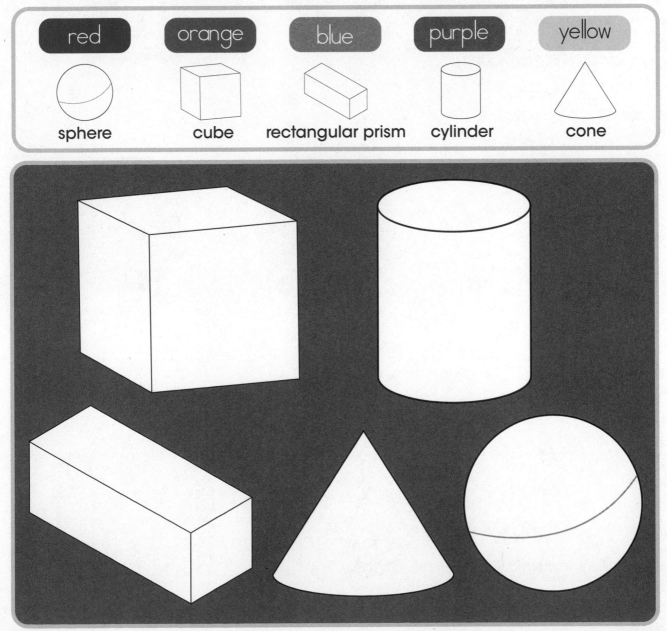

red	orange	blue	purple	yellow
sphere	cube	rectangular prism	cylinder	cone

Geometry

2-Dimensional and 3-Dimensional Shapes

Circle the 2-dimensional shapes with a red crayon.

Circle the 3-dimensional shapes with a blue crayon.

Making a Tally Mark Table

Tally marks can be used to show how many of each item there are.

Example: $||||$ = 4 and $\cancel{||||}$ = 5 and $\cancel{||||}$ $|$ = 6

Count the fruit and fill in the graph using tally marks.

Fruit Market

Type of Fruit	Tally Marks	Number
Apple	$\cancel{||||}$	5
Orange		
Banana		
Watermelon		

Use the table to answer the questions below.

Which fruit has the least tally marks? _____

Which fruit has the most tally marks? _____

How many fruits are there in all? _____

Creating a Bar Graph

Each tally mark represents one insect.

Color in the number of units needed to match the tally marks for each insect on the bar graph.

Summer Insects

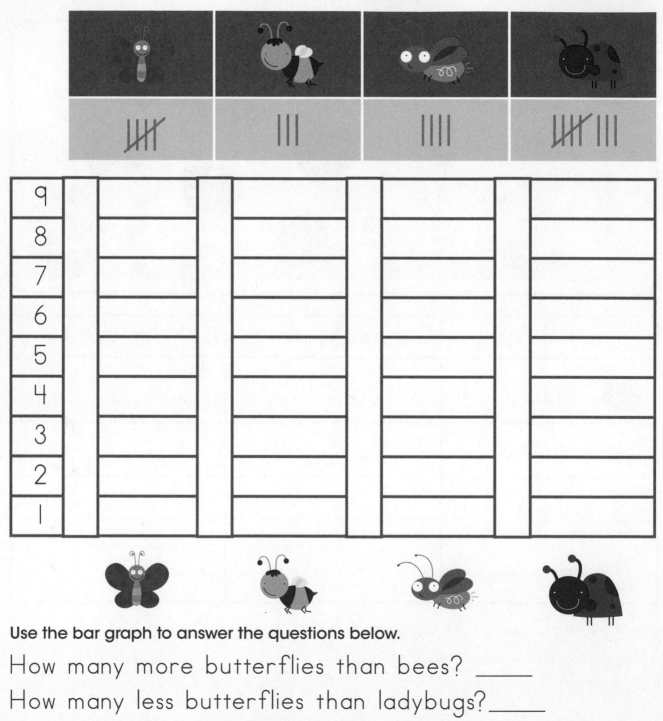

Use the bar graph to answer the questions below.

How many more butterflies than bees? _____

How many less butterflies than ladybugs? _____

How many bees and fireflies are there all together? _____

180

Creating a Bar Graph

Each student in this first grade class picked their favorite treats. Complete the bar graph by coloring the correct number of boxes for each treat.

Our Favorite Treats

Which treat is the class favorite? _____

Graphing Shapes

Color in the graph to show how many of each shape is in the picture below.

Shapes

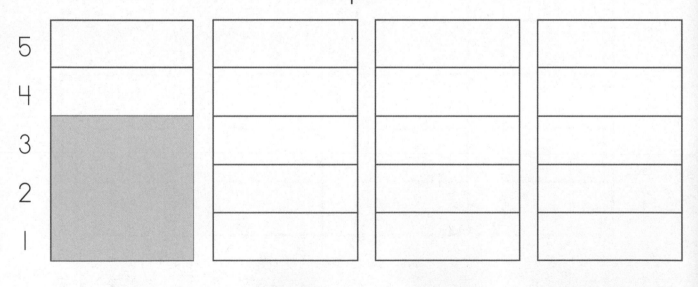

Sorting and Categorizing

Reading a Bar Graph

Each colored section represents one person who likes that sport. Count how many votes each sport received and answer the questions below.

How many people like football?_____

How many people like soccer?_____

How many people like basketball?_____

How many people like baseball?_____

Our Favorite Sports

CERTIFICATE
of Achievement

....

has successfully completed
1st Grade Math

Date: ....

Signed: ....

Extra Practice Pages

Table of Contents

Pencil Practice

Practice writing the uppercase and lowercase letters on the lines below.

A a

Write the word ant.

Draw a picture of something that begins with the letter A.

Color the pictures that begin with the letter A.

Pencil Practice

Practice writing the uppercase and lowercase letters on the lines below.

Write the word bat.

Draw a picture of something that begins with the letter B.

Circle the picture that begins with the letter B.

Pencil Practice

Practice writing the uppercase and lowercase letters on the lines below.

C c

Write the word cow.

Draw a picture of something that begins with the letter C.

Circle the picture that begins with the letter C.

Pencil Practice

Practice writing the uppercase and lowercase letters on the lines below.

Dd

Write the word doll.

Draw a picture of something that begins with the letter D.

Color the pictures that begin with the letter D.

Pencil Practice

Practice writing the uppercase and lowercase letters on the lines below.

Write the word elf.

Draw a picture of something that begins with the letter E.

Color the pictures that begin with the letter E.

Practice writing the uppercase and lowercase letters on the lines below.

Write the word fan.

Draw a picture of something that begins with the letter F.

Circle the picture that begins with the letter F.

Practice writing the uppercase and lowercase letters on the lines below.

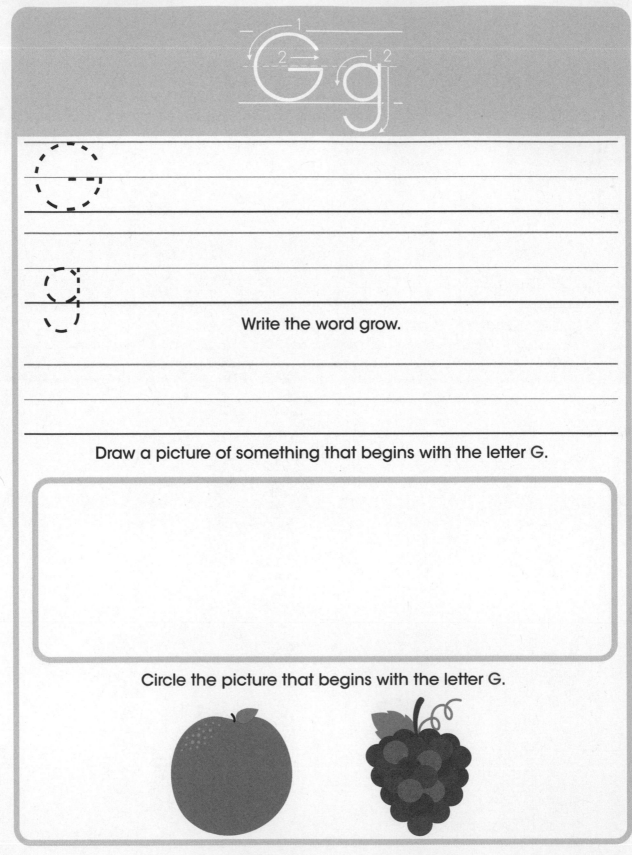

Write the word grow.

Draw a picture of something that begins with the letter G.

Circle the picture that begins with the letter G.

Practice writing the uppercase and lowercase letters on the lines below.

Write the word happy.

Draw a picture of something that begins with the letter H.

Color the pictures that begin with the letter H.

Pencil Practice

Practice writing the uppercase and lowercase letters on the lines below.

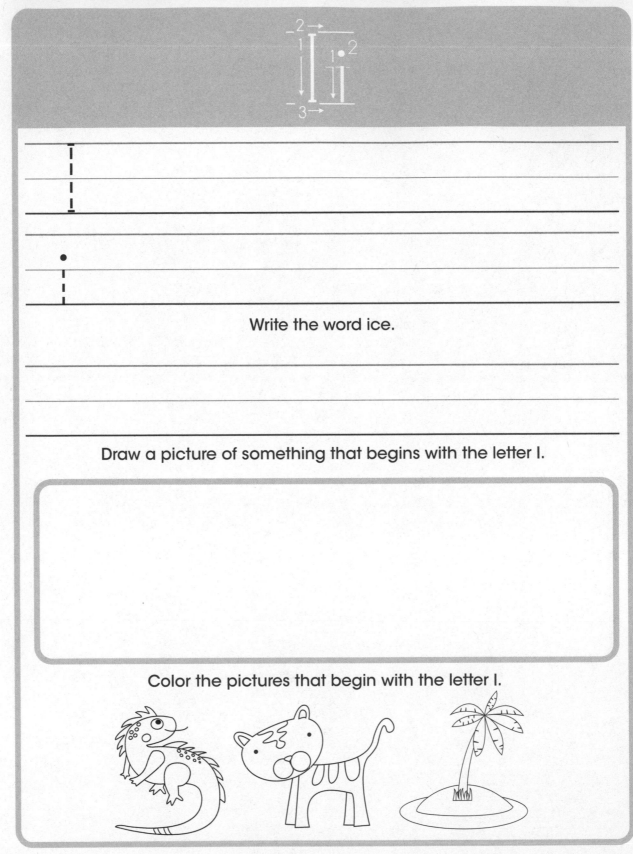

Write the word ice.

Draw a picture of something that begins with the letter I.

Color the pictures that begin with the letter I.

Practice writing the uppercase and lowercase letters on the lines below.

Write the word jar.

Draw a picture of something that begins with the letter J.

Circle the picture that begins with the letter J.

Pencil Practice

Practice writing the uppercase and lowercase letters on the lines below.

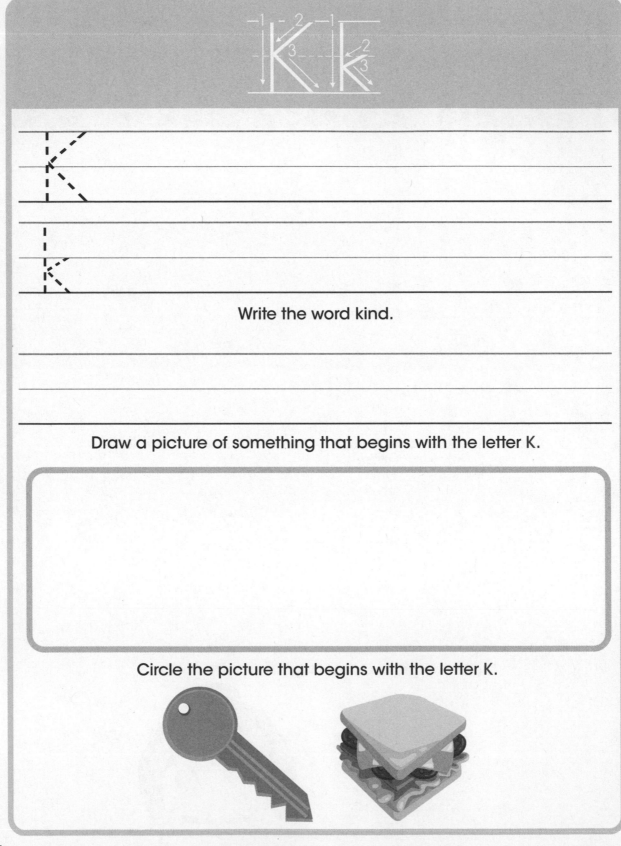

Write the word kind.

Draw a picture of something that begins with the letter K.

Circle the picture that begins with the letter K.

Pencil Practice

Practice writing the uppercase and lowercase letters on the lines below.

Write the word love.

Draw a picture of something that begins with the letter L.

Color the pictures that begin with the letter L.

Practice writing the uppercase and lowercase letters on the lines below.

M m

M

m

Write the word moose.

Draw a picture of something that begins with the letter M.

Color the pictures that begin with the letter M.

Practice writing the uppercase and lowercase letters on the lines below.

Write the word nice.

Draw a picture of something that begins with the letter N.

Circle the picture that begins with the letter N.

Pencil Practice

Practice writing the uppercase and lowercase letters on the lines below.

Write the word owl.

Draw a picture of something that begins with the letter O.

Circle the picture that begins with the letter O.

Practice writing the uppercase and lowercase letters on the lines below.

P   p

P _____

P _____

Write the word pig.

_____

_____

Draw a picture of something that begins with the letter P.

Color the pictures that begin with the letter P.

Pencil Practice

Practice writing the uppercase and lowercase letters on the lines below.

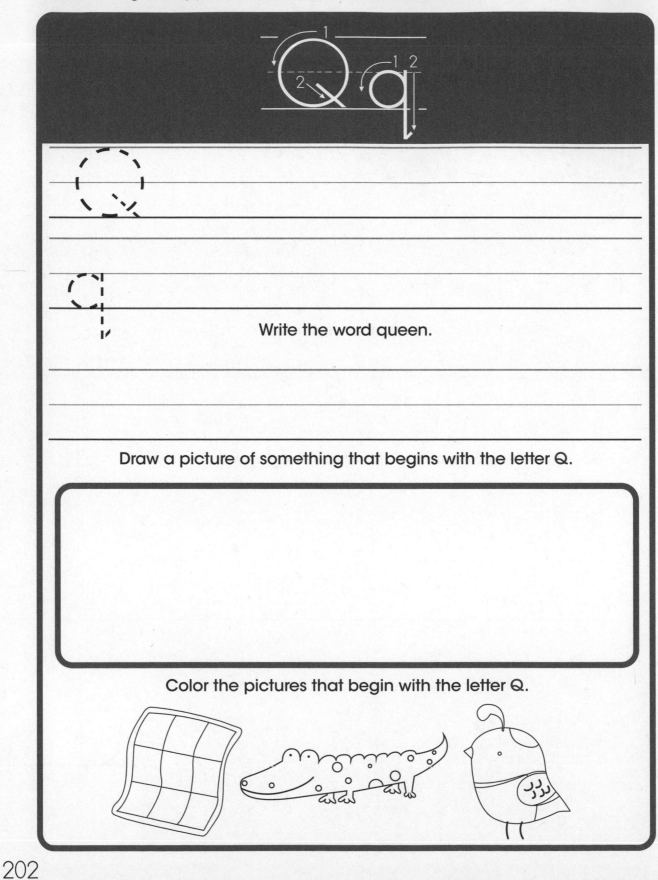

Write the word queen.

Draw a picture of something that begins with the letter Q.

Color the pictures that begin with the letter Q.

Practice writing the uppercase and lowercase letters on the lines below.

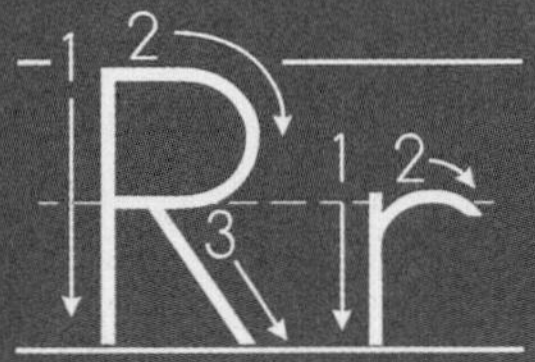

R r

R

r

Write the word rain.

Draw a picture of something that begins with the letter R.

Circle the picture that begins with the letter R.

Pencil Practice

Practice writing the uppercase and lowercase letters on the lines below.

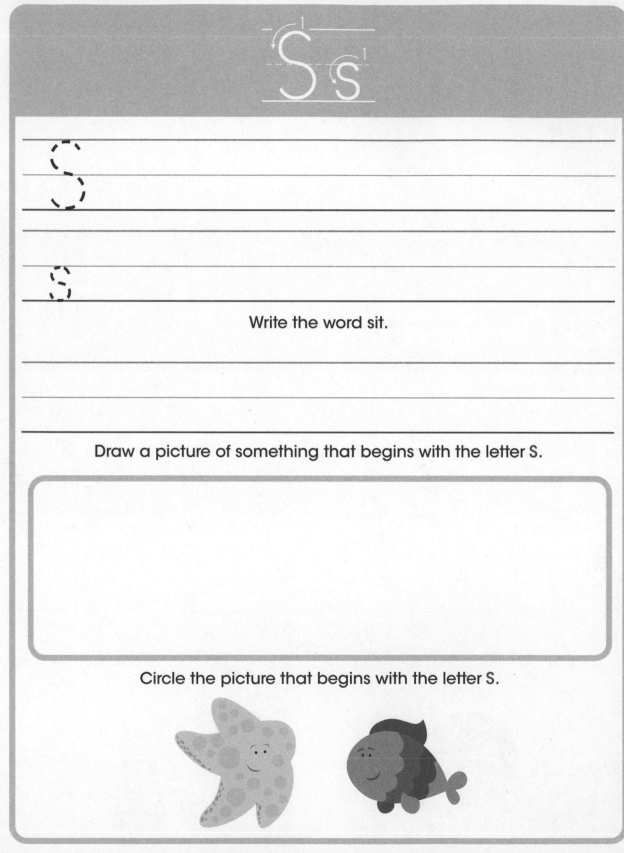

Write the word sit.

Draw a picture of something that begins with the letter S.

Circle the picture that begins with the letter S.

Pencil Practice

Practice writing the uppercase and lowercase letters on the lines below.

Write the word tiger.

Draw a picture of something that begins with the letter T.

Color the pictures that begin with the letter T.

Practice writing the uppercase and lowercase letters on the lines below.

Uu

Write the word under.

Draw a picture of something that begins with the letter U.

Color the pictures that begin with the letter U.

Practice writing the uppercase and lowercase letters on the lines below.

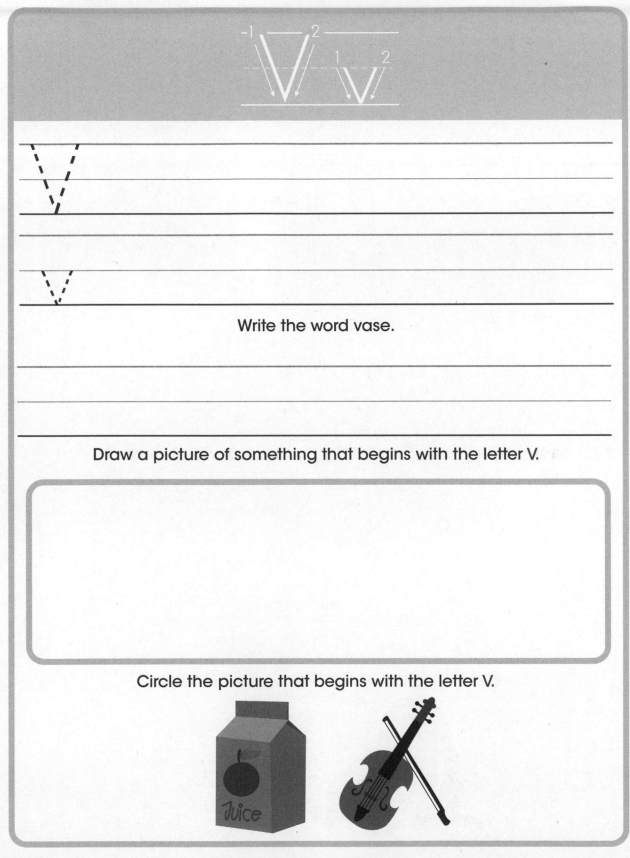

Write the word vase.

Draw a picture of something that begins with the letter V.

Circle the picture that begins with the letter V.

Pencil Practice

Practice writing the uppercase and lowercase letters on the lines below.

W W

Write the word wood.

Draw a picture of something that begins with the letter W.

Circle the picture that begins with the letter W.

Pencil Practice

Practice writing the uppercase and lowercase letters on the lines below.

Write the word x-ray.

Draw a picture of something that begins with the letter X.

Color the picture that begins with the letter X.

Pencil Practice

Practice writing the uppercase and lowercase letters on the lines below.

Write the word yellow.

Draw a picture of something that begins with the letter Y.

Color the pictures that begin with the letter Y.

Pencil Practice

Practice writing the uppercase and lowercase letters on the lines below.

Z z

Write the word zero.

Draw a picture of something that begins with the letter Z.

Circle the picture that begins with the letter Z.

211

Reading Strategies

When you get stuck on a word, use a reading strategy to help you figure the word out. Write the missing sounds to complete the words.

STRATEGY: Say the beginning sound.

_____og

_____nake

_____ee

_____ion

_____rab

_____ish

When you get stuck on a word, use a reading strategy to help you figure the word out. Write the missing sound's letter to complete each word.

STRATEGY: Stretch out the sounds.

b_____t

b_____s

k_____te

w_____gon

b_____d

c_____p

Super Sight Words

Some words are difficult to sound out and do not have picture clues.
Reading and remembering them can make reading easier.
Practice reading the sight words below.

the	no	look	came
is	like	so	down
in	my	do	them
it	what	she	would
to	were	an	could
I	when	said	went
he	come	can	her
at	have	not	am
be	some	but	get
we	into	up	want
all	his	here	your
had	as	little	will
saw	on	make	about
this	for	yes	many
they	see	then	look
with	you	out	very
are	a	will	has
was	and	go	from
that	of	if	use
by	or	there	first

Super Sight Words

Roll a die and use the key to write the corresponding sight words in the correct column. Roll until the grid is full.

 down   went    many   about   from   saw

Roll a Sight Word					

Writers write using their imagination. Become a writer by thinking about the sentence starters below and writing what you picture in your mind.

On my birthday...

_____

_____

At school I like to...

_____

_____

When I grow up...

_____

_____

I wish I had...

_____

_____

My favorite food is...

_____

_____

Look at the picture. What is happening? Write about it on the lines below.

Know Your Numbers

Count the objects below and write the number below each set. Be a careful counter! Touch each object as you count it to be sure you don't miscount!

9

_____

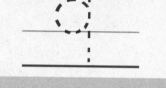
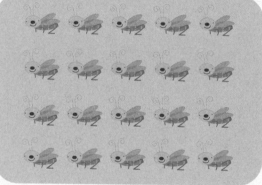

_____

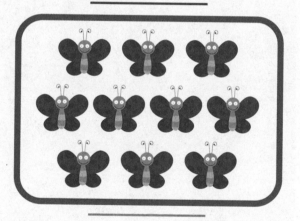

_____

_____

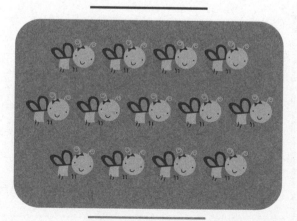

_____

Know Your Numbers

Count the objects below and write the number below each set. Be a careful counter! Touch each object as you count it to be sure you don't miscount!

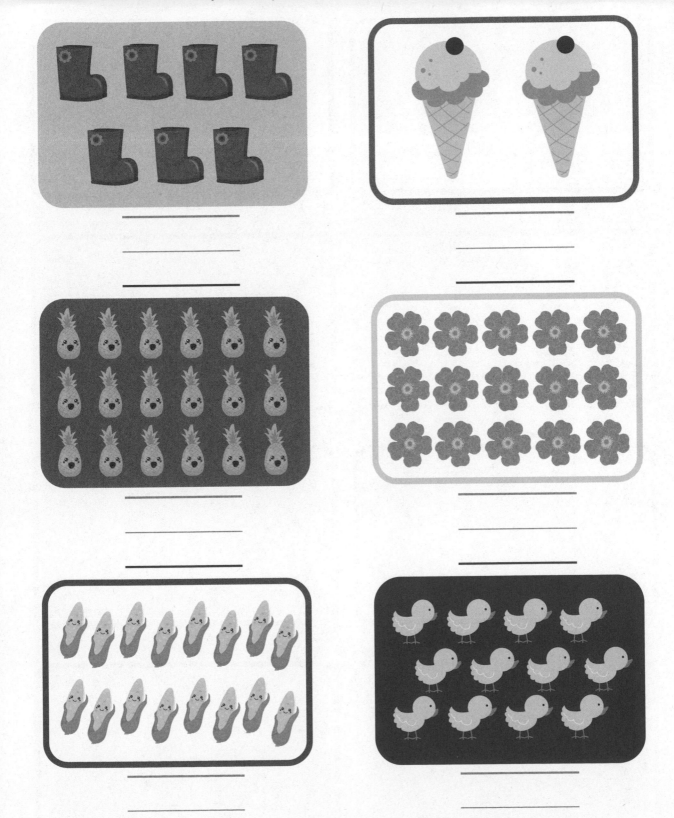

219

Math Practice

Use some of the strategies that you have practiced (counting tallies, counting pictures, or number lines) to solve these equations. Write the sums on the lines.

$10 + 1 =$ _____

$2 + 8 =$ _____

$4 + 7 =$ _____

$8 + 1 =$ _____

$9 + 3 =$ _____

$8 + 4 =$ _____

$3 + 6 =$ _____

$6 + 6 =$ _____

Use some of the strategies that you have practiced (counting tallies, counting pictures, or number lines) to solve these equations. Write the sums on the lines.

6 + 1 = _____

7 + 4 = _____

3 + 7 = _____

4 + 8 = _____

Count the circles on Max's top and write the number on the first line. Count the circles on Max's pants and write the number on the second line. How may circles are there in all? Write the sum on the last line. Now color Max's pajamas.

_____ + _____ = _____

Math Practice

Use some of the strategies that you have practiced (counting tallies, counting pictures, or number lines) to solve these equations. Write the sums on the lines.

16 - 8 = _____

7 - 6 = _____

13 - 8 = _____

13 - 3 = _____

12 - 3 = _____

10 - 1 = _____

12 - 10 = _____

12 - 6 = _____

Use some of the strategies that you have practiced (counting tallies, counting pictures, or number lines) to solve these equations. Write the sums on the lines.

11 - 9 = ____

15 - 4 = ____

19 - 11 = ____

18 - 9 = ____

Pictures can also be great tools to help you add. Count the pictures that represent the numbers in the equations. Then write each number and the sum on the lines.

Example:

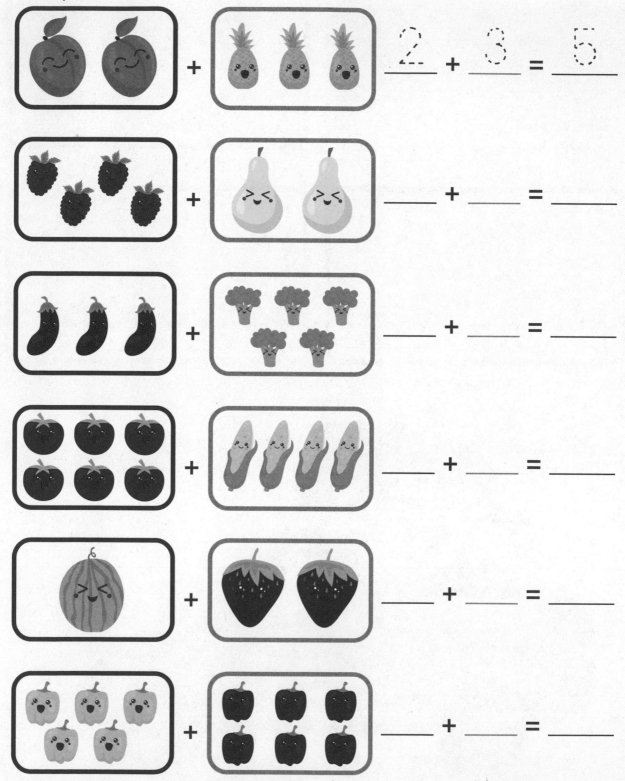

$\underline{2} + \underline{3} = \underline{5}$

$\underline{} + \underline{} = \underline{}$

$\underline{} + \underline{} = \underline{}$

$\underline{} + \underline{} = \underline{}$

$\underline{} + \underline{} = \underline{}$

$\underline{} + \underline{} = \underline{}$

Use the dots on the dominoes to help you add. Write the equations to match the domino dots. Then solve the equation and write the sums on the lines below.

Example:

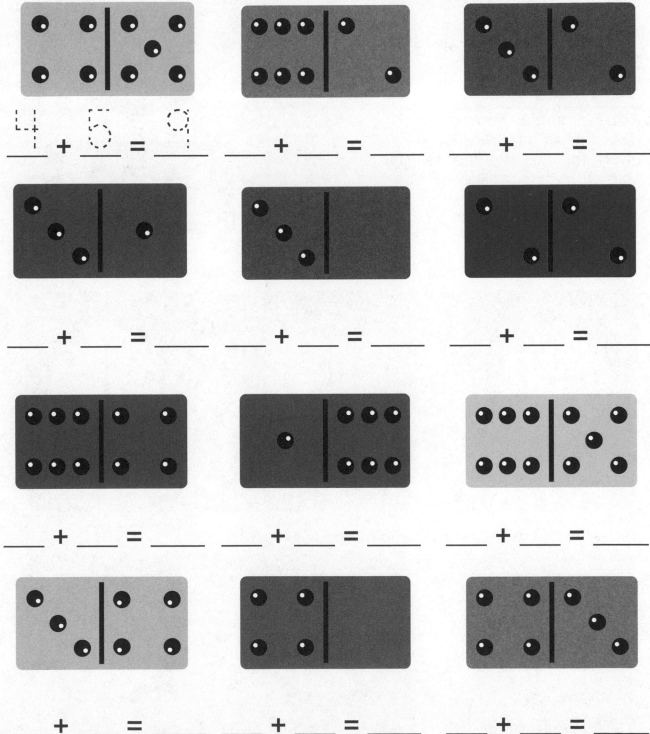

4 + 5 = 9
___ + ___ = ___   ___ + ___ = ___   ___ + ___ = ___

___ + ___ = ___   ___ + ___ = ___   ___ + ___ = ___

___ + ___ = ___   ___ + ___ = ___   ___ + ___ = ___

___ + ___ = ___   ___ + ___ = ___   ___ + ___ = ___

What Time is it?

This is an analog clock.

It has a long hand and a short hand.
It has the numbers 1-12 located on the face of
the clock. The long hand points
to the minute and the short hand points
to the hour. This clock says 5 o'clock.

This is a digital clock.

The first number shows the hour and the
second two numbers tell how
many minutes after the hour it is.
This clock says 3 o'clock.

hour   minutes

What time is it? Write the digital time under each clock.

4:00

Draw the hands on the clocks to match the digital times.

5:00   8:00   11:00

What Time is it?

What time is it? Write the digital time under each clock.

2:30

Draw the hands on the clocks to match the digital times.

10:30   5:30   1:30

Draw a line to connect the digital time to the matching analog clock.

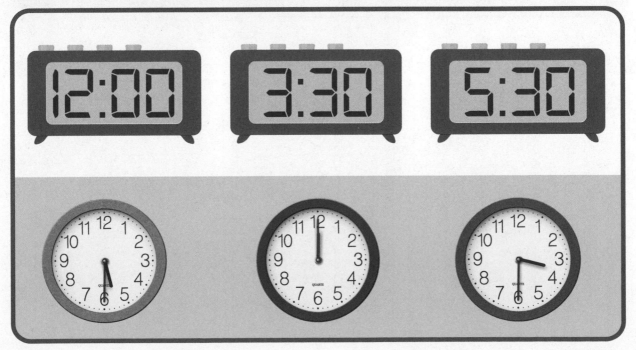

ANSWER KEY

Page 7

Decoding Strategies

Look at the Pictures
A word is missing in each sentence below. Read the sentences and use the pictures as clues to help you decide what each missing word is. Circle the correct missing word and write it on the lines below.

The cat is up the **tree**
(tree or top)

The boy has a **sandwich**
(shoe or sandwich)

I like to play **soccer**
(baseball or soccer)

My mom likes to **cook**
(cook or jump)

She is riding the **bike**
(bus or bike)

Page 8

Decoding Strategies

Picture Clues
A word is missing in each sentence below. Read the sentences and use the pictures as clues to help you decide what each missing word is. Circle the correct missing word and write it on the lines below.

I saw **animals** at the zoo.
(fish or animals)

I saw **pigs** at the farm.
(pigs or lions)

I had an **apple** for lunch.
(orange or apple)

I take the **bus** to school.
(bus or canoe)

I had a birthday **cake**
(chair or cake)

Page 9

Decoding Strategies

Initial Sounds
Look at the pictures. Write the missing letters to complete the words below. Then read the words.

b_oy   r_un   p_ig

b_aby   t_able   c_at

_letter   f_rog   g_oat

Page 10

Decoding Strategies

Initial Sounds
Read the words in the pictures below.
Color the flowers with words that begin with the letter j.

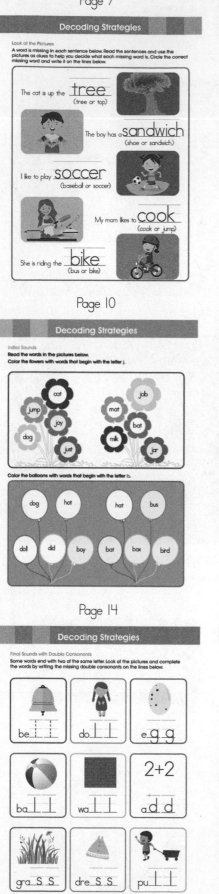

cat   job   jump   mat   joy   bat   dog   milk   just   jar

Color the balloons with words that begin with the letter b.

dog   hot   hat   bus   doll   dd   boy   bat   box   bird

Page 11

Decoding Strategies

Medial Sounds
Look at the pictures. Write the missing letters to complete the words below.

b_e_d   h_a_t   h_e_n

c_a_t   n_e_t   l_o_g

s_u_n   t_o_p   b_u_s

Page 12

Decoding Strategies

Medial Sounds
Write the missing vowels to complete each word below. Then draw a line to match the object on the left to its opposite on the right.

li_ttle   h_o_t

s_u_mmer   w_i_nter

c_o_ld   l_o_ng

sh_o_rt   b_i_g

Page 14

Decoding Strategies

Final Sounds with Double Consonants
Some words end with two of the same letter. Look at the pictures and complete the words by writing the missing double consonants on the lines below.

be_ll_   do_ll_   e_gg_

ba_ll_   wa_ll_   a_dd_

gra_ss_   dre_ss_   pu_ll_

Page 15

Decoding Strategies

Looking for "Chunks"
Recognizing parts of words can help you sound out words faster. Look for "chunks" in the words you read. Circle the words below that have the chunk shown on the left.

Chunk			
sh	(share)	chick	(show)
ch	(chip)	(chin)	this
th	(that)	when	(there)
at	shop	(mat)	(bat)
an	(man)	(tan)	cat
ack	(rack)	barn	(sack)
ip	top	(sip)	(slip)
ill	(bill)	(fill)	fall
op	(mop)	him	(stop)
ut	(hut)	hit	(nut)

Page 16

Decoding Strategies

Flipping the Vowel
Long Vowel Sounds
Write the missing vowels to complete each story. Then read the stories.

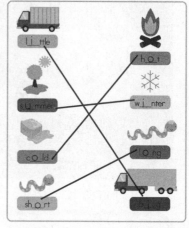

Come out to pl_a_y.

It is a sunny d_a_y.

What do you s_a_y?

I grew out of my tr_i_ke.

I now have a b_i_ke.

It is what I l_i_ke.

Page 17

Decoding Strategies

Context Clues and Picture Clues

Sometimes trying to figure out a word by sounding it out may not help you. If this happens, try skipping the word and reading the rest of the sentence to see if you can figure out the word. Does the sentence sound right? Does it make sense? Another clue to help you figure out an unknown word is to look at the pictures on the page you are reading.

A word is missing in each sentence below. Read the sentences. Use the other words in the sentences and the pictures to help you figure out the missing words. Write the missing words on the lines below.

The _frog_ is on the log.

I can ride a _bike_.

I see a cow near the _barn_.

The cat has a red _hat_.

I can climb a _tree_.

Page 19

Sight Word Activities

Sight Words

Find and circle the sight words below using different colors for each word. Then fill in the graph by coloring one box for every sight word you find. Write the total number of words you find next to the graph on the lines below.

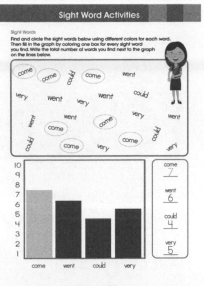

come	7
went	6
could	4
very	5

Page 20

Sight Word Activities

Sight Words

Color the pumpkins below using the key.

when =   look =   said =
all =   by =

Page 21

Sight Word Activities

Sight Words

Color the picture below using the key.

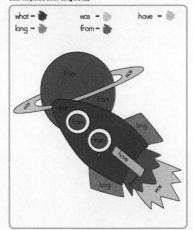

what -   was -   have -
long -   from -

Page 23

Sight Word Activities

Sight Words

Complete the word search below by finding and circling all the sight words listed in the box. Words may be horizontal, vertical, or diagonal, but they will all be forwards—no backwards words allowed! Search for the following words:

| and | out | make | in | it |
| my | she | about | this | if |

O	E	H	K	T	H	I	S	C	H	K
U	B	C	G	A	G	P	G	R	I	M
T	C	B	A	H	K	B	O	N	C	N
F	D	C	G	M	J	I	T	A	L	C
I	B	H	A	E	A	P	S	W	A	X
H	E	T	N	I	B	K	C	V	F	U
O	M	E	D	F	R	S	E	N	K	E
F	B	F	G	P	Q	H	M	A	L	G
N	R	A	N	J	O	E	D	I	G	J
O	A	W	L	G	S	I	F	X	Y	Z
M	Y	I	J	Q	B	K	O	F	C	I
O	A	B	O	U	T	F	L	E	I	X

Page 26

Rhymes and Rhyming Words

Words That Rhyme

Words that rhyme have the same ending sound. Circle the words that rhyme. Then color the pictures.

Page 27

Rhymes and Rhyming Words

Words That Rhyme

Circle the words that rhyme. Then color the picture.

Page 28

Vocabulary

Word Meanings

Read the story below.

Halloween Night

It was raining on Halloween night. I was feeling disappointed. I had a great monster costume. I got dressed up anyway. I jumped out and surprised my dad and frightened him. Finally, the rain stopped and my dad took me trick-or-treating.

Read the questions below about the story and circle the correct answers.

In the story, the word "disappointed" means:
a. scared   b. happy   (c. sad)

The word "frightened" means:
a. happy   (b. scared)   c. sad

The word "finally" means:
(a. at last)   b. first   c. before

Page 29

Vocabulary

Word Meanings

Read the story below.

The Circus

I can't believe it happened! I was at the circus with my mom. A tiger let out a huge roar. The magician was doing tricks. Then a clown picked me out of the audience to help. The magician made me disappear!

Read the questions below about the story and circle the correct answers.

In the story, the word "huge" means:
a. small   (b. very big)   c. tiny

The word "audience" means:
a. a loud noise   (b. people watching a show)   c. tired

The word "disappear" means:
a. turn purple   (b. can't be seen)   c. get really hungry

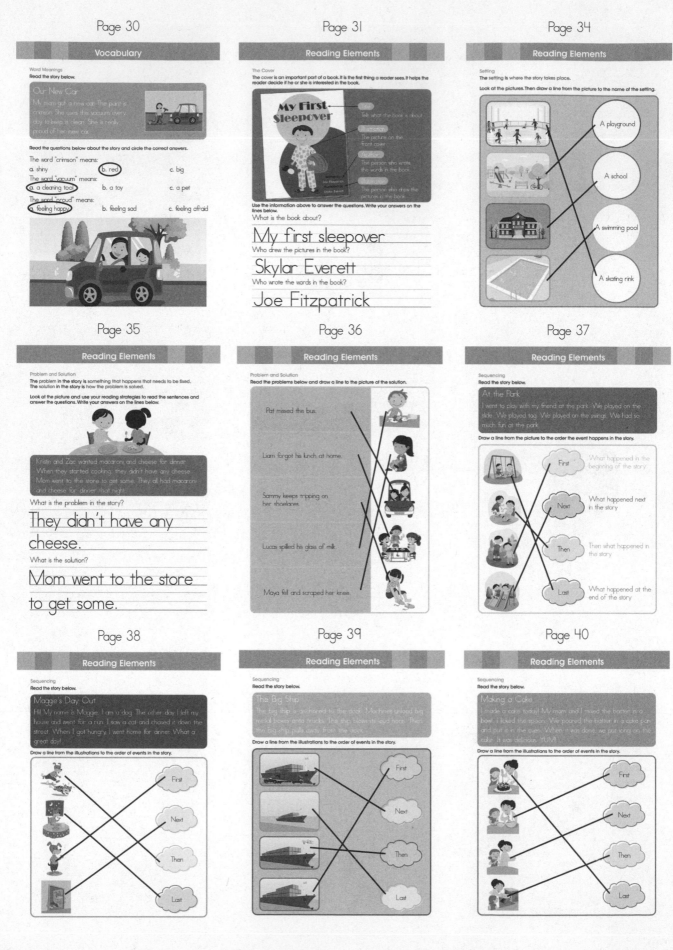

Page 42

Making Predictions
Use the cover to make predictions about the book. Draw a line from the book cover to your prediction.

- Kids riding bikes
- A day at school
- Animals in a forest

- Whales in the ocean
- A camping trip
- Soccer practice

Page 50

Understanding What You Read Using Clues
Look at each picture and read the sentences. Circle the sentence that matches the picture and then rewrite it on the lines below.

The boy is making a cake.
The girl is painting the fence.

The girl is painting the fence.

The farmer is milking the cow.
The man is chopping down the tree.

The farmer is milking the cow.

The pig is in the barn.
The horse jumped over the fence.

The pig is in the barn.

The girl is reading a book.
The boys are playing tag.

The boys are playing tag.

Page 51

Understanding What You Read Using Clues
Use the clues to find out who each character is. Draw a line from the character to his or her name.

Connor is wearing a red shirt. He likes to play soccer.
Gabby plays with her baby doll.
Max loves to read.
Kate loves to pick flowers.

- Max
- Gabby
- Kate
- Connor

Page 52

Understanding What You Read Using Clues
Read the sentences and color the picture that matches the clues.

I walk sideways.
I have claws.

I love to go for walks and play fetch.

I have four legs.

I live on a farm.
I make milk.

I love to eat carrots.

I have long ears.

Page 53

Understanding What You Read Using Clues
Read the sentences below.

Hannah is wearing a pink top. Jane is wearing a green skirt with a green top. Jane always wears a bow in her hair to match her top. Ben has curly hair and is wearing a blue sweater and blue jeans. Kurt has brown hair and it is the same color as his jacket. Jacob has red hair that matches his favorite shoes.

Color the picture to match the sentences. Then, on the lines below, answer the questions about what you read.

How many kids are waiting for the school bus? five
Who is first in line? Jacob
Who is last in line? Ben

Page 54

Following Directions
Read the directions below and color the picture.

1. Color the bush to the left of the house green.
2. Color the sun yellow.
3. Color the chimney on the roof red.
4. Color the windows light blue.
5. Draw some fluffy clouds in the sky.
6. Draw three flowers near the tree.
7. Color the door red.
8. Color the leaves on the tree green.
9. Color the rest of the house any color you like.

Page 60

Riddles
Riddles are brain teasers that make you think. Read the riddles below and try to answer them. Then color the pictures.

1. I am full of holes, but I can still hold water.
   What am I? sponge
2. I have hands and a face, but I can't touch or smile.
   What am I? clock
3. I get wetter and wetter the more I dry.
   What am I? towel
4. I have lots of keys but can't open any door.
   What am I? piano

Page 61

Compound Words
Compound words are two words that when combined make a new word when they are put together. Look at the pictures to figure out the compound words. Write the words on the lines below.

- + = football
- + = toothbrush
- + = sunflower
- + = rainbow
- + = cupcake

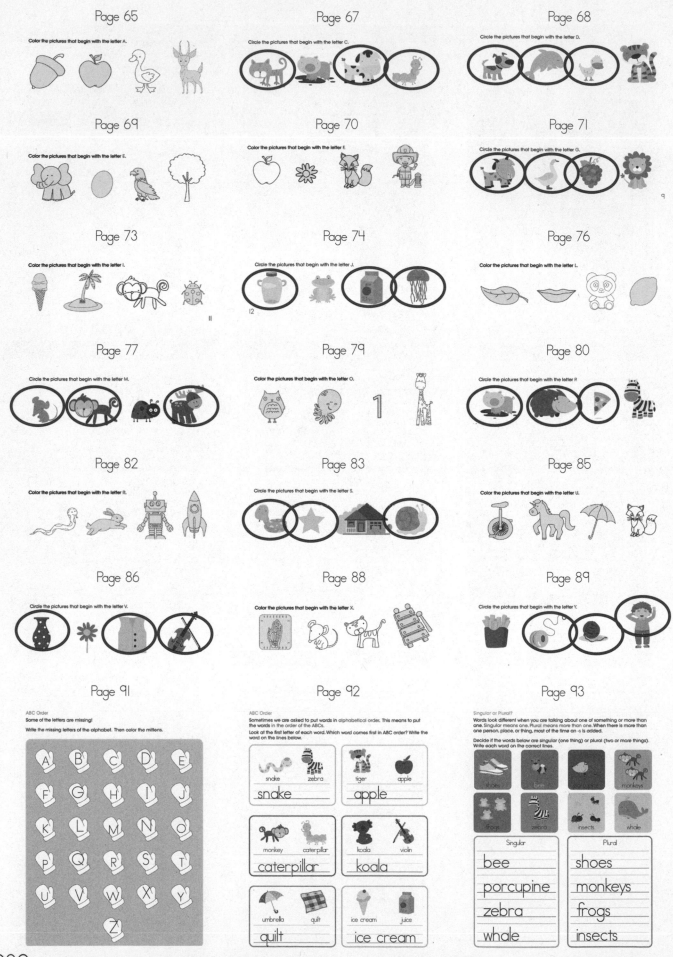

Page 65

Color the pictures that begin with the letter A.

Page 67

Circle the pictures that begin with the letter C.

Page 68

Circle the pictures that begin with the letter D.

Page 69

Color the pictures that begin with the letter E.

Page 70

Color the pictures that begin with the letter F.

Page 71

Circle the pictures that begin with the letter G.

9

Page 73

Color the pictures that begin with the letter I.

11

Page 74

Circle the pictures that begin with the letter J.

12

Page 76

Color the pictures that begin with the letter L.

Page 77

Circle the pictures that begin with the letter M.

Page 79

Color the pictures that begin with the letter O.

1

Page 80

Circle the pictures that begin with the letter P.

Page 82

Color the pictures that begin with the letter R.

Page 83

Circle the pictures that begin with the letter S.

Page 85

Color the pictures that begin with the letter U.

Page 86

Circle the pictures that begin with the letter V.

Page 88

Color the pictures that begin with the letter X.

Page 89

Circle the pictures that begin with the letter Y.

Page 91

ABC Order

Some of the letters are missing!

Write the missing letters of the alphabet. Then color the mittens.

A B C D E
F G H I J
K L M N O
P Q R S T
U V W X Y
Z

Page 92

ABC Order

Sometimes we are asked to put words in alphabetical order. This means to put the words in the order of the ABCs.

Look at the first letter of each word. Which word comes first in ABC order? Write the word on the lines below.

snake zebra
snake

tiger apple
apple

monkey caterpillar
caterpillar

koala violin
koala

umbrella quilt
quilt

ice cream juice
ice cream

Page 93

Singular or Plural?

Words look different when you are talking about one of something or more than one. Singular means one. Plural means more than one. When there is more than one person, place, or thing, most of the time an -s is added.

Decide if the words below are singular (one thing) or plural (two or more things). Write each word on the correct lines.

shoes   bee   porcupine   monkeys
frogs   zebra   insects   whale

Singular	Plural
bee	shoes
porcupine	monkeys
zebra	frogs
whale	insects

232

Page 94

Grammar and Punctuation

Contractions

Contractions are two words made into one word.
An apostrophe is placed where some of the letters are removed.

Example: cannot becomes can't

Draw a line from the two words to its matching contraction.

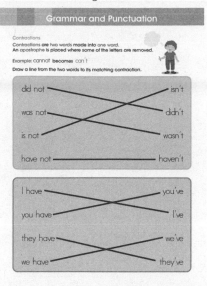

did not — didn't
was not — wasn't
is not — isn't
have not — haven't

I have — I've
you have — you've
they have — we've
we have — they've

Page 95

Grammar and Punctuation

Contractions

Draw a line from the words to the correct contractions.

I will — I'll
you will — you'll
they will — she'll
she will — they'll

I am — I'm
he is — he's
she is — she's
it is — it's
who is — who's

Page 96

Grammar and Punctuation

Sentences

Every sentence starts with a capital letter and ends with a punctuation mark.
Statement sentences tell the reader something. They start with a capital letter
and end with a period.

This is a period .

Something is missing! Read the statement sentences and correct them on the lines
below. Start with a capital letter and end with a period.

i like to read
I like to read.

you are my friend
You are my friend.

the glass is full
The glass is full.

that dog is brown
That dog is brown.

i see a bird
I see a bird.

Page 97

Grammar and Punctuation

Sentences

Question sentences ask someone something. They start with a capital letter and
end with a question mark.

This is a question mark ?

Something is missing! Read the question sentences and correct them on the lines
below. Start with a capital letter and end with a question mark.

can you play with me
Can you play with me?

may I have a juice box
May I have a juice box?

do you like ice cream
Do you like ice cream?

how do you ride a bike
How do you ride a bike?

will you walk the dog
Will you walk the dog?

Page 98

Grammar and Punctuation

Sentences

Exclamation sentences either tell someone to do something or express
excitement. They start with a capital letter and end with an exclamation mark.

This is an exclamation mark !

Something is missing! Read the exclamation sentences and correct them on the
lines below. Start with a capital letter and end with an exclamation mark.

look up at the bird
Look up at the bird!

hooray, we won
Hooray, we won!

ouch, that hurts
Ouch, that hurts!

i found my shoes
I found my shoes!

i can help
I can help!

Page 100

Grammar and Punctuation

Fix the Sentences

Look at the sentences below. There is something missing.

Read the sentences and circle the mistakes in red. Then rewrite the sentences
below with capital letters and the correct punctuation.

Example: (i)t is time for bed()   It is time for bed.

(i) can brush my teeth ()
I can brush my teeth.

(l)et's go to the park ()
Let's go to the park.

(o)uch, I hurt my finger ()
Ouch, I hurt my finger!

(d)o you have a pet ()
Do you have a pet?

(h)ow fast can you run ()
How fast can you run?

(y)ou are my best friend ()
You are my best friend.

Page 101

Grammar and Punctuation

Nouns

Nouns are words for people, animals, places, and things.

Color the nouns in the gumball machine using the key. Then color the rest of
the picture.

person = red   animal = blue
place = yellow   thing = green

chair, park, office, book, school, store, bird, dog, cat, fish

Page 102

Grammar and Punctuation

Verbs

Verbs are words that tell what a noun is doing. They are action words.

Circle the verb in each sentence. Color the pictures.

That girl is (waving).   The boy (ran) to the park.

My teacher (reads) a book.   Your mom (bakes) a cake.

The dog (chases) the cat.   The bird (flew) away.

I can (jump) rope.   The bunny is (hopping).

Page 103

Grammar and Punctuation

Adjectives

Adjectives describe something. They tell how it looks, feels, smells, tastes, or sounds.

Read the words in each row. Circle the two words that describe the picture.

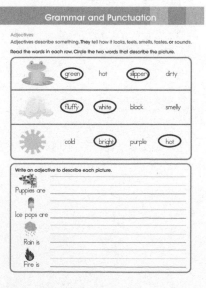

(green)   hot   (slippery)   dirty

(fluffy)   white   black   smelly

cold   (bright)   purple   (hot)

Write an adjective to describe each picture.

Puppies are ____
Ice pops are ____
Rain is ____
Fire is ____

233

Page 128

Counting 1-10
Count the pictures in each box and write the total number on the lines below.

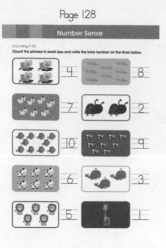

4   8
7   2
10 9
6   3
5   1

Page 130

Counting 11-20
Count the pictures in each box and write the total number on the lines below.

15 18
13 14
20 19
17 12
16 11

Page 131

Number Words
Draw a line from the number word to the matching number.

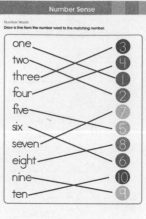

one
two
three
four
five
six
seven
eight
nine
ten

3 4 1 2 7 5 8 6 10 9

Page 133

Counting 51-100
Connect the dots from 51 to 100.
Color your new friend when you're finished.

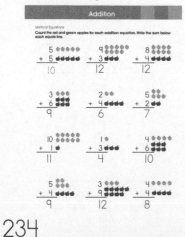

Page 135

Count by Twos
Skip counting can make counting faster! Skip counting means skipping numbers as you count.

Circle groups of 2 objects while you skip count the pictures in each row. Write the number on the lines for how many you counted in each row.

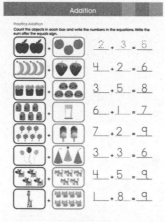

4
6
8
10
12
14

Page 137

Count by Tens
Count 10 objects at a time. Circle sets of 10 objects while you skip count the objects in each row. Write the number on the lines for how many you counted in each row.

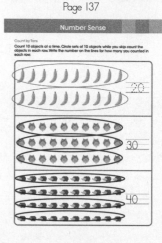

20
30
40

Page 138

Count by Tens
Count 10 objects at a time. Circle sets of 10 objects while you skip count the pictures in each row. Write the number on the lines for how many you counted in each row.

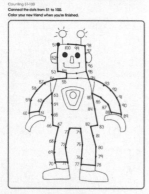

60
70
80
90

Page 139

Practice Addition
Count the objects in each box and write the numbers in the equations. Write the sum after the equals sign.

$2 + 3 = 5$
$4 + 2 = 6$
$3 + 5 = 8$
$6 + 1 = 7$
$7 + 2 = 9$
$3 + 3 = 6$
$4 + 5 = 9$
$1 + 8 = 9$

Page 140

Let's Play Dominoes!
Count the dots on each side of the domino and write the numbers in the equations. Write the sum after the equals sign.

$5 + 5 = 10$ $2 + 6 = 8$ $3 + 3 = 6$
$4 + 6 = 10$ $6 + 1 = 7$ $6 + 5 = 11$
$5 + 3 = 8$ $2 + 1 = 3$ $3 + 6 = 9$
$5 + 4 = 9$ $6 + 4 = 10$ $2 + 4 = 6$

16

Page 141

Vertical Equations
Count the red and green apples for each addition equation. Write the sum below each equals line.

$5 + 5 = 10$ $9 + 3 = 12$ $8 + 4 = 12$
$3 + 6 = 9$ $2 + 4 = 6$ $5 + 2 = 7$
$10 + 1 = 11$ $1 + 3 = 4$ $4 + 6 = 10$
$5 + 4 = 9$ $3 + 9 = 12$ $4 + 4 = 8$

Page 142

Using a Number Line
You can use a number line to help you count when adding.
Start on the number line at the first number in the equation. Then jump forward the number of spaces for the amount being added to the first number. Circle the number on the number line where the jump line ends. This is the sum. Write the sum after the equals sign.

$8 + 2 = 10$
$2 + 4 = 6$
$7 + 1 = 8$
$3 + 2 = 5$
$6 + 4 = 10$
$3 + 6 = 9$
$3 + 4 = 7$
$5 + 3 = 8$

Page 143

Using a Number Line
Start on the first number in the equation. Then jump forward on the line the same number of spaces as the second number. Draw a line from the first number to the second number and circle the correct answer. Then write the answers to the equations on the lines below.

$6 + 3 = 9$
$4 + 6 = 10$
$9 + 1 = 10$
$4 + 4 = 8$
$5 + 2 = 7$
$2 + 6 = 8$
$4 + 5 = 9$
$4 + 3 = 7$

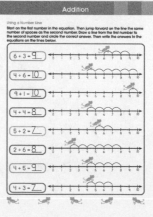
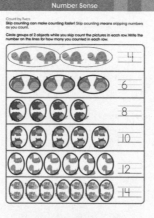

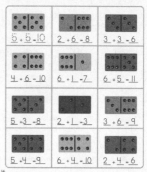

Page 144

Addition

Sunny Summer Math
Solve the addition equations and write the sums on the lines below. Then color the pictures.

$4 + 8 = 12$ $4 + 6 = 10$ $5 + 6 = 11$
$9 + 3 = 12$ $6 + 6 = 12$ $5 + 7 = 12$
$9 + 1 = 10$ $5 + 1 = 6$ $8 + 3 = 11$
$7 + 5 = 12$ $9 + 2 = 11$ $7 + 4 = 11$
$6 + 2 = 8$ $1 + 6 = 7$ $6 + 3 = 9$ $10 + 2 = 12$
$11 + 1 = 12$ $4 + 4 = 8$ $8 + 5 = 13$ $3 + 8 = 11$

Page 145

Addition

Word Problems
Sometimes math equations are hidden in story problems. Read each addition story problem carefully and figure out the unknown number to solve the equation. Write that number on the line in each equation.

Example: Maddy has 2 red beads. She got 3 more beads from a friend. How many beads does Maddy have now?

$2 + 3 = \underline{5}$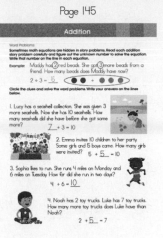

Circle the clues and solve the word problems. Write your answers on the lines below.

1. Lucy has a seashell collection. She was given 3 more seashells. Now she has 10 seashells. How many seashells did she have before she got some more?
$\underline{7} + 3 = 10$

2. Emma invites 10 children to her party. Some girls and 5 boys came. How many girls were invited?
$5 + \underline{5} = 10$

3. Sophia likes to run. She runs 4 miles on Monday and 6 miles on Tuesday. How far did she run in two days?
$4 + 6 = \underline{10}$

4. Noah has 2 toy trucks. Luke has 7 toy trucks. How many more toy trucks does Luke have than Noah?
$2 + \underline{5} = 7$

Page 146

Addition

Add to the Fun
Solve the addition problems. Write the answers below.

2 +9 11	3 +4 7	2 +6 8	3 +8 11	2 +7 9
7 +8 15	6 +4 10	1 +9 10	5 +11 16	10 +12 22
5 +12 17	3 +5 8	4 +5 9	0 +7 7	5 +9 14
8 +12 20	3 +10 13			
7 +12 19	1 +10 11			
0 +9 9	4 +5 9			

Page 147

Addition

Word Problems
Read each addition story problem carefully and figure out the unknown number to solve the equation. Write that number on the line in each equation.

1. Sarah has 5 test tubes. She has 3 yellow and the rest are red. How many test tubes are red?
$3 + \underline{2} = 5$

2. Lauren has 4 T-shirts with a red heart on them. She has 5 T-shirts with a dog on them. How many T-shirts does she own?
$4 + 5 = \underline{9}$

3. Ashley has 8 shoes. She has 6 shoes with laces and the rest have buttons. How many shoes have buttons?
$6 + \underline{2} = 8$

4. Kim painted her nails. She has 3 fewer pink nails than blue nails on her hands. How many blue nails does she have?
$\underline{7} + 3 = 10$

Page 149

Subtraction

Practice Subtraction
Subtracting is taking away part of a whole number. When we use pictures to subtract, we start with the whole number and then cross out the number of objects we are subtracting.

Example: $6 - 2 = 4$ ●●●●XX

Count the total number of objects in each row. Count backward for the amount of the second number in the equation, starting from the right equation. (This will be the X objects). The number of objects left is the difference. Write the difference under the equals line.

$\frac{8}{-4}{\ \ 4}$

$\frac{8}{-6}{\ \ 2}$

$\frac{10}{-4}{\ \ 6}$

$\frac{7}{-3}{\ \ 4}$

$\frac{5}{-4}{\ \ 1}$

$\frac{8}{-2}{\ \ 6}$

Page 150

Subtraction

Practice Subtraction
Cross out the number of objects you are subtracting from the total. Count the objects left and write the difference after the equals sign.

$9 - 3 = \underline{6}$ $10 - 4 = \underline{6}$

$7 - 6 = \underline{1}$ $12 - 7 = \underline{5}$

$9 - 7 = \underline{2}$ $14 - 10 = \underline{4}$

$6 - 3 = \underline{3}$ $11 - 8 = \underline{3}$

26

Page 151

Subtraction

Practice Subtraction
Cross out the number of objects you are subtracting from the total. Count the objects left and write the difference after the equals sign.

$8 - 3 = \underline{5}$ $5 - 4 = \underline{1}$

$7 - 5 = \underline{2}$ $9 - 2 = \underline{7}$

$6 - 3 = \underline{3}$ $8 - 5 = \underline{3}$

$7 - 2 = \underline{5}$ $6 - 2 = \underline{4}$

Page 152

Subtraction

Let's Play Dominoes!
Use the dots on the dominoes to help you subtract. Write the difference for each equation after the equals sign.

$12 - 6 = \underline{6}$ $9 - 4 = \underline{5}$ $10 - 6 = \underline{4}$

$11 - 6 = \underline{5}$ $8 - 2 = \underline{6}$ $6 - 3 = \underline{3}$

$7 - 1 = \underline{6}$ $10 - 5 = \underline{5}$ $8 - 5 = \underline{3}$

$7 - 3 = \underline{4}$ $8 - 4 = \underline{4}$ $6 - 2 = \underline{4}$

Page 153

Subtraction

Word Problems
Sometimes math equations are hidden in story problems. Read each subtraction story problem carefully and figure out the unknown number to solve the equation. Write that number on the line in each equation.

Example: Maddy said there were 5 apples on the table. She ate some. Now there are 2 apples. How many did Maddy eat?
$5 - \underline{3} = 2$

Circle the clues and solve the word problems. Write your answers on the lines below.

1. Juan has 5 trading cards. He gave 2 away as gifts. How many does he still have?
$5 - 2 = \underline{3}$

2. Oliver popped 4 balloons at the party. Mason popped 8 balloons. How many fewer balloons did Oliver pop than Mason?
$8 - 4 = \underline{4}$

3. Logan has some drums on Monday. He gave 5 drums away on Tuesday. Now he has 4 drums. How many drums did he have on Monday?
$\underline{9} - 5 = 4$

4. Hannah has 4 fewer sheep than Riley. Riley has 7 sheep. How many sheep does Hannah have?
$7 - 4 = \underline{3}$

Page 154

Subtraction

Using a Number Line
You can use a number line to help you count when subtracting. Start on the number line at the first number in the equation. Then, jump backward the number of spaces for the amount being taken away from the first number. Circle the number on the number line where the jump line ends. This is the difference. Write the difference after the equals sign.

Example
$9 - 6 = 3$
$6 - 2 = \underline{4}$
$5 - 4 = \underline{1}$
$4 - 1 = \underline{3}$
$3 - 3 = \underline{0}$
$6 - 5 = \underline{1}$
$8 - 4 = \underline{4}$
$7 - 5 = \underline{2}$
$9 - 2 = \underline{7}$

Page 155

Subtraction

Using a Number Line
Start on the number line at the first number in the equation. Then, jump backward the number of spaces for the amount being taken away from the first number. Circle the number on the number line where the jump line ends. Write the difference after the equals sign.

$7 - 6 = \underline{1}$
$8 - 6 = \underline{2}$
$8 - 7 = \underline{1}$
$9 - 7 = \underline{2}$
$7 - 2 = \underline{5}$
$9 - 5 = \underline{4}$
$5 - 2 = \underline{3}$
$6 - 2 = \underline{4}$
$8 - 1 = \underline{7}$

Page 156

Subtraction

Math Can Be a Picnic!
Solve the subtraction equations and write the differences after the equals signs.

$10 - 4 = 6$ $12 - 8 = 4$ $15 - 6 = 9$ $10 - 8 = 2$
$16 - 7 = 9$ $18 - 9 = 9$ $14 - 7 = 7$ $12 - 2 = 10$
$12 - 4 = 8$ $11 - 7 = 4$ $15 - 9 = 6$ $18 - 10 = 8$
$15 - 8 = 7$ $11 - 2 = 9$ $17 - 9 = 8$ $16 - 0 = 16$
$12 - 7 = 5$ $17 - 8 = 9$ $13 - 7 = 6$ $18 - 0 = 18$
$14 - 5 = 9$ $12 - 3 = 9$ $16 - 9 = 7$ $9 - 7 = 2$

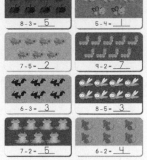

235

Subtraction

Word Problems
Read each subtraction story problem carefully and figure out the unknown number to solve the equation. Write that number on the line in each equation.

1. Avery has 10 students in her class. Some students went to the nurse. Now she has 3 students. How many children are not feeling well?

$10 - \underline{7} = 3$

2. Emily has 4 tomatoes. Lily has 8 tomatoes. How many fewer tomatoes does Emily have than Lily?

$8 - 4 = \underline{4}$

3. Connor has 9 tents. He has 3 brown tents and the rest are green. How many tents are green?

$9 - 3 = \underline{6}$

4. Trevor has some canoes for rent. He rents 2 out in the afternoon. Now he has 5 canoes. How many did he have in the morning?

$\underline{7} - 2 = 5$

Subtraction

Vertical Equations
Solve the subtraction equations. Write the differences below the equals lines.

12 − 2 = 10	12 − 3 = 9	10 − 1 = 9	11 − 4 = 7	12 − 6 = 7
10 − 2 = 8	9 − 4 = 5	12 − 7 = 5	8 − 5 = 3	11 − 1 = 10
10 − 8 = 2	7 − 6 = 1	12 − 4 = 8	3 − 1 = 2	8 − 4 = 4
4 − 0 = 4	8 − 2 = 6	7 − 4 = 3	9 − 0 = 9	6 − 2 = 4
12 − 8 = 4				5 − 1 = 4

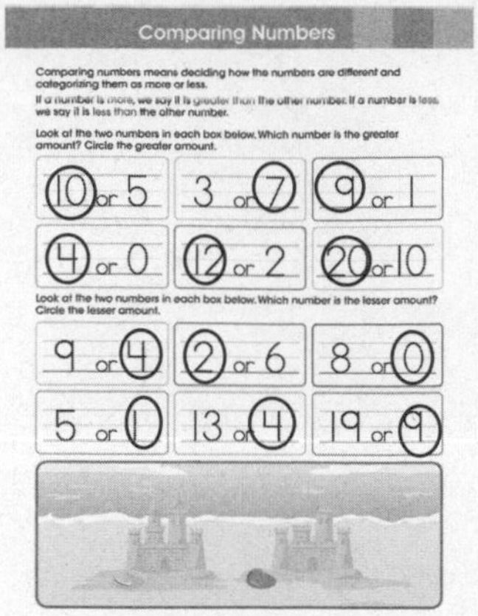

Comparing Numbers

Comparing numbers means deciding how the numbers are different and categorizing them as more or less.
If a number is more, we say it is greater than the other number. If a number is less, we say it is less than the other number.
Look at the two numbers in each box below. Which number is the greater amount? Circle the greater amount.

⑩ or 5	3 or ⑦	⑨ or 1
④ or 0	⑫ or 2	⑳ or 10

Look at the two numbers in each box below. Which number is the lesser amount? Circle the lesser amount.

9 or ④	② or 6	8 or ⓪
5 or ①	13 or ④	19 or ⑨

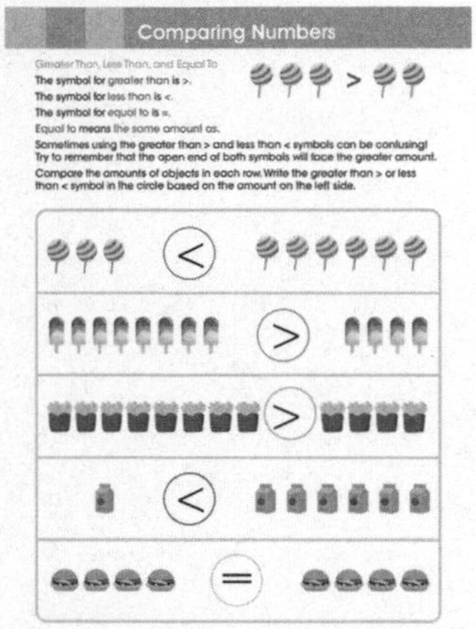

Comparing Numbers

Greater Than, Less Than, and Equal To
The symbol for greater than is >.
The symbol for less than is <.
The symbol for equal to is =.
Equal to means the same amount as.
Sometimes using the greater than > and less than < symbols can be confusing. Try to remember that the open end of both symbols will face the greater amount.
Compare the amounts of objects in each row. Write the greater than > or less than < symbol in the circle based on the amount on the left side.

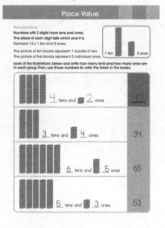

Equal Shares

Equal Shares
Equal shares are parts of a whole. Equal shares must be the same size.
Example:

equal   not equal

Color the shapes below that have equal shares.

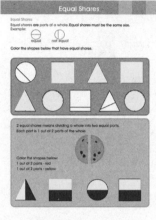

2 equal shares means dividing a whole into two equal parts.
Each part is 1 out of 2 parts of the whole.

Color the shapes below:
1 out of 2 parts - red
1 out of 3 parts - yellow

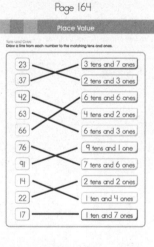

Equal Shares

One Fourth

One fourth or ¼ means cutting a whole into four equal parts.
Each part is ¼ of the whole.

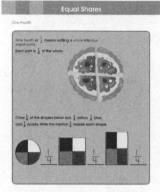

Color ¼ of the shapes below red, ¼ yellow, ¼ blue, and ¼ purple. Write the fraction ¼ beside each shape.

$\frac{1}{4}$ $\frac{1}{4}$ $\frac{1}{4}$

Place Value

Tens and Ones
Numbers with 2 digits have tens and ones.
The place of each digit tells which one it is.
Example: 15 = 1 ten and 5 ones.

The picture of ten blocks represent 1 bundle of ten.
The picture of five blocks represent 5 individual ones.

1 ten   5 ones

Look at the illustrations below and write how many tens and how many ones are in each group. Then, use those numbers to write the totals in the boxes.

_4_ tens and _2_ ones   42

_3_ tens and _4_ ones   34

_6_ tens and _5_ ones   65

_5_ tens and _3_ ones   53

Place Value

Tens and Ones
Draw a line from each number to the matching tens and ones.

23	3 tens and 7 ones
37	2 tens and 3 ones
42	6 tens and 6 ones
63	4 tens and 2 ones
66	6 tens and 3 ones
76	9 tens and 1 one
91	7 tens and 6 ones
14	2 tens and 2 ones
22	1 ten and 4 ones
17	1 ten and 7 ones

Place Value

Tens and Ones
Write how many tens and ones are in each number on the lines below.

21 = _2_ tens and _1_ one   54 = _5_ tens and _4_ ones
15 = _1_ ten and _5_ ones   73 = _7_ tens and _3_ ones
24 = _2_ tens and _4_ ones   52 = _5_ tens and _2_ ones
42 = _4_ tens and _2_ ones   19 = _1_ ten and _9_ ones
81 = _8_ tens and _1_ one   11 = _1_ ten and _1_ one
66 = _6_ tens and _6_ ones   34 = _3_ tens and _4_ ones
                               53 = _5_ tens and _3_ ones

Measurement

Length
We can measure the length of something in two ways.
We can use a nonstandard form of measurement, such as a paper clip or a stacking cube, or we can use a standard form of measurement, such as such as a ruler, which measures in inches.
Measure the items below with a nonstandard form of measurement and write the lengths on the lines below.

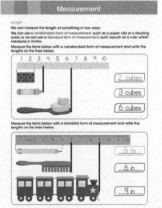

2 cubes
3 cubes
6 cubes

Measure the items below with a standard form of measurement and write the lengths on the lines below.

5 in
6 in
9 in

Measurement

Longer and Shorter
Circle the objects that are longer. Cross out the objects that are shorter.

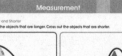
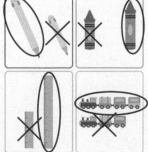

Measurement

Bigger and Smaller
Circle the objects that are bigger. Cross out the objects that are smaller.

236

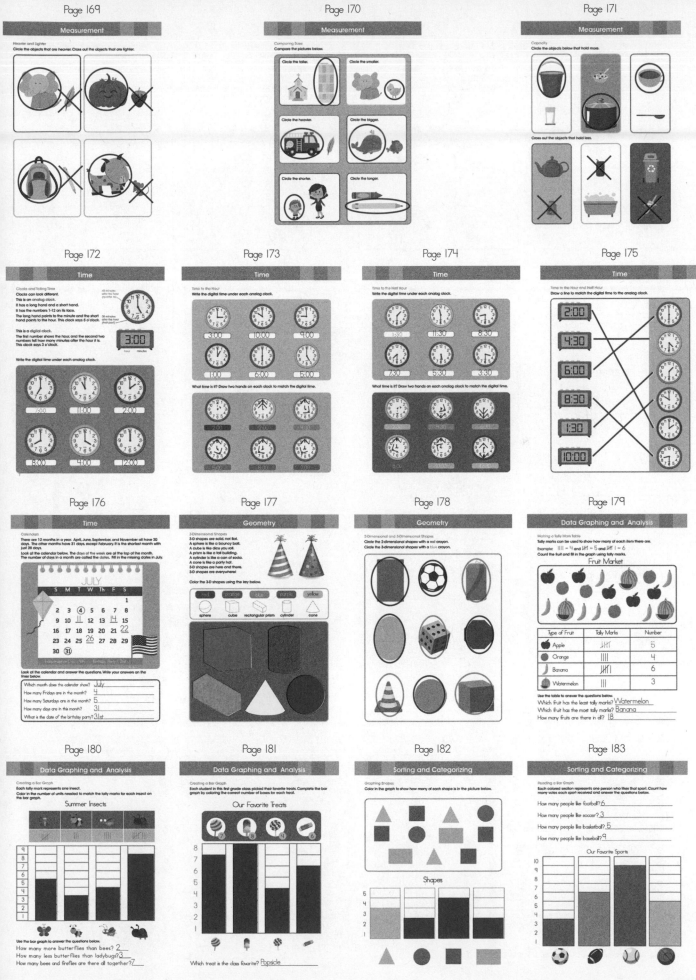

237

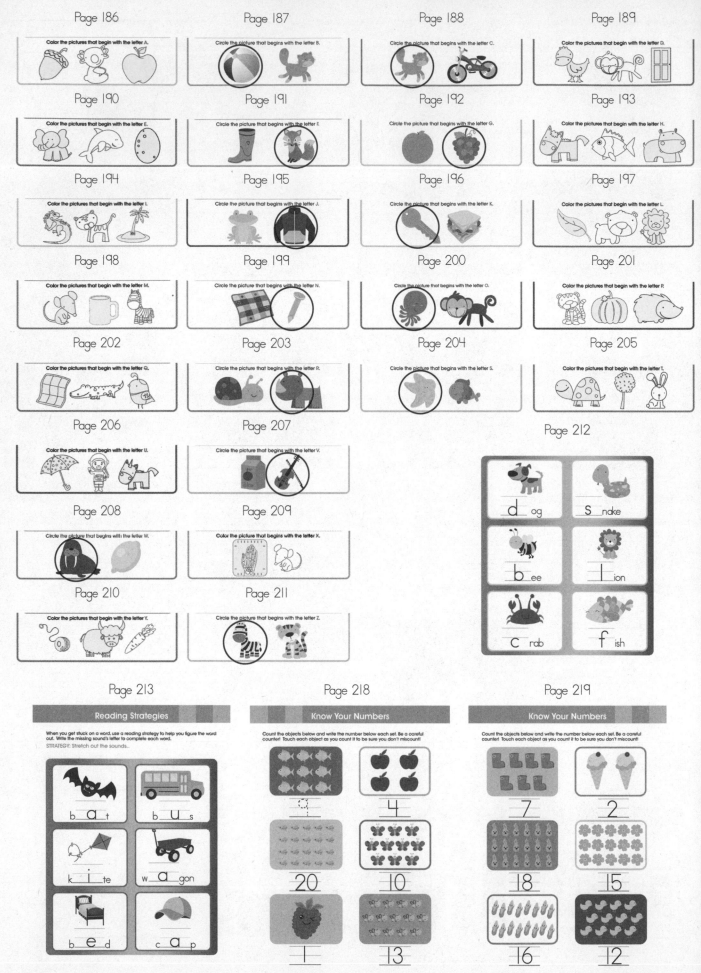

Page 186 — Color the pictures that begin with the letter A.
Page 187 — Circle the picture that begins with the letter B.
Page 188 — Circle the picture that begins with the letter C.
Page 189 — Color the pictures that begin with the letter D.
Page 190 — Color the pictures that begin with the letter E.
Page 191 — Circle the picture that begins with the letter F.
Page 192 — Circle the picture that begins with the letter G.
Page 193 — Color the pictures that begin with the letter H.
Page 194 — Color the pictures that begin with the letter I.
Page 195 — Circle the picture that begins with the letter J.
Page 196 — Circle the picture that begins with the letter K.
Page 197 — Color the pictures that begin with the letter L.
Page 198 — Color the pictures that begin with the letter M.
Page 199 — Circle the picture that begins with the letter N.
Page 200 — Circle the picture that begins with the letter O.
Page 201 — Color the pictures that begin with the letter P.
Page 202 — Color the pictures that begin with the letter Q.
Page 203 — Circle the picture that begins with the letter R.
Page 204 — Circle the picture that begins with the letter S.
Page 205 — Color the pictures that begin with the letter T.
Page 206 — Color the pictures that begin with the letter U.
Page 207 — Circle the picture that begins with the letter V.
Page 208 — Circle the picture that begins with the letter W.
Page 209 — Color the picture that begins with the letter X.
Page 210 — Color the pictures that begin with the letter Y.
Page 211 — Circle the picture that begins with the letter Z.

Page 212
d og   s nake
b ee   l ion
c rab   f ish

Page 213
Reading Strategies
When you get stuck on a word, use a reading strategy to help you figure the word out. Write the missing sound's letter to complete each word.
STRATEGY: Stretch out the sounds..
b a t   b u s
k i te   w a gon
b e d   c a p

Page 218
Know Your Numbers
Count the objects below and write the number below each set. Be a careful counter! Touch each object as you count it to be sure you don't miscount!
9   4
20   10
1   13

Page 219
Know Your Numbers
Count the objects below and write the number below each set. Be a careful counter! Touch each object as you count it to be sure you don't miscount!
7   2
18   15
16   12

238

Page 220

Math Practice

Use some of the strategies that you have practiced (counting tallies, counting pictures, or number lines) to solve these equations. Write the sums on the lines.

$10 + 1 = 11$ $2 + 8 = 10$

$4 + 7 = 11$ $8 + 1 = 9$

$9 + 3 = 12$ $8 + 4 = 12$

$3 + 6 = 9$ $6 + 6 = 12$

Page 221

Math Practice

Use some of the strategies that you have practiced (counting tallies, counting pictures, or number lines) to solve these equations. Write the sums on the lines.

$6 + 1 = 7$ $7 + 4 = 11$

$3 + 7 = 10$ $4 + 8 = 12$

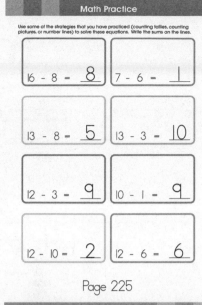

Count the circles on Max's top and write the number on the first line. Count the circles on Max's pants and write the number on the second line. How many circles are there in all? Write the sum on the last line. Now color Max's pajamas.

$6 + 5 = 11$

Page 222

Math Practice

Use some of the strategies that you have practiced (counting tallies, counting pictures, or number lines) to solve these equations. Write the sums on the lines.

$16 - 8 = 8$ $7 - 6 = 1$

$13 - 8 = 5$ $13 - 3 = 10$

$12 - 3 = 9$ $10 - 1 = 9$

$12 - 10 = 2$ $12 - 6 = 6$

Page 223

Math Practice

Use some of the strategies that you have practiced (counting tallies, counting pictures, or number lines) to solve these equations. Write the sums on the lines.

$11 - 9 = 2$ $15 - 4 = 11$

$19 - 11 = 8$ $18 - 9 = 9$

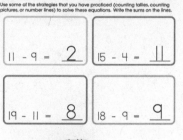

Page 224

Math Practice

Pictures can also be great tools to help you add. Count the pictures that represent the numbers in the equations. Then write each number and the sum on the lines.

Example:

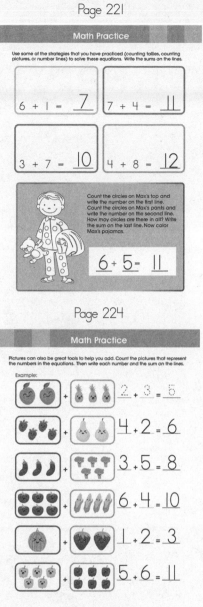

$2 + 3 = 5$

$4 + 2 = 6$

$3 + 5 = 8$

$6 + 4 = 10$

$1 + 2 = 3$

$5 + 6 = 11$

Page 225

Math Practice

Use the dots on the dominoes to help you add. Write the equations to match the domino dots. Then solve the equation and write the sums on the lines below.

Example:

$4 + 5 = 9$ $6 + 2 = 8$ $3 + 2 = 5$

$3 + 1 = 4$ $3 + 0 = 3$ $2 + 2 = 4$

$6 + 4 = 10$ $1 + 6 = 7$ $6 + 5 = 11$

$3 + 4 = 7$ $4 + 0 = 4$ $4 + 3 = 7$

Page 226

What Time is it?

This is an analog clock.
It has a long hand and a short hand.
It has the numbers 1-12 located on the face of the clock. The long hand points to the minute and the short hand points to the hour. This clock says 5 o'clock.

This is a digital clock.
The first number shows the hour and the second two numbers tell how many minutes after the hour it is.
This clock says 3 o'clock.

3:00
hour   minutes

What time is it? Write the digital time under each clock.

3:00   4:00   6:00

Draw the hands on the clocks to match the digital times.

5:00   8:00   11:00

Page 227

What Time is it?

What time is it? Write the digital time under each clock.

2:30   7:30   3:30

Draw the hands on the clocks to match the digital times.

10:30   5:30   1:00

Draw a line to connect the digital time to the matching analog clock.

12:00   3:30   5:30

Build Solid Foundations for Learning

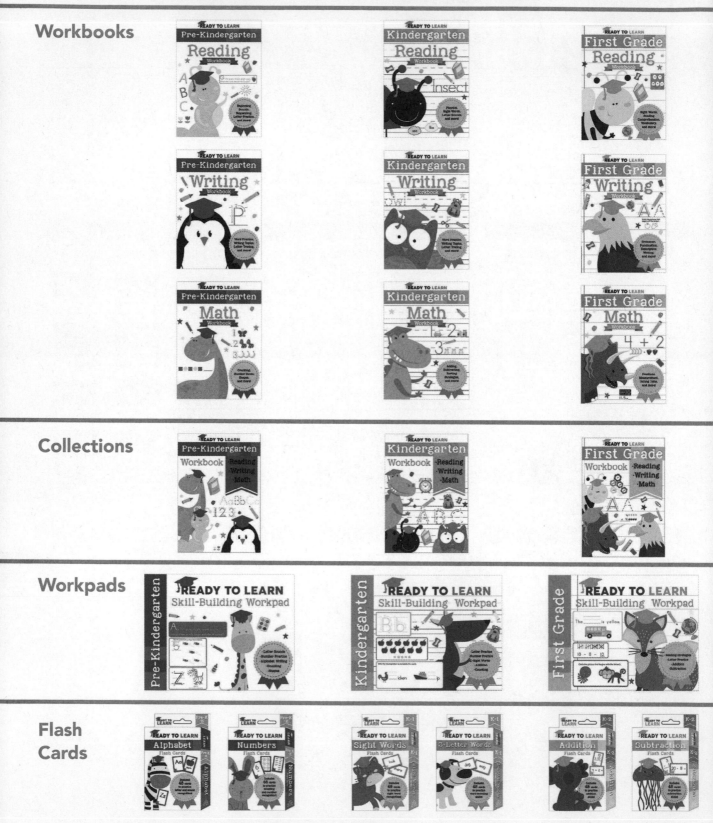

Workbooks

Collections

Workpads

Flash Cards